Captured Landscape

The enclosed garden, or *hortus conclusus*, is a place where architecture, architectural elements, and landscape come together. It has a long history, ranging from the paradise garden and cloister, the botanic garden and the *giardino segreto*, the kitchen garden and the stage for social display, to its many modern forms; the city retreat, the redemptive garden, and the deconstructed building. By its nature it is ambiguous. Is it an outdoor room, or captured landscape? Is it garden or architecture?

Kate Baker discusses the continuing relevance of the typology of the enclosed garden to contemporary architects by exploring influential historical examples alongside some of the best of contemporary designs – brought to life with vivid photography and detailed drawings – taken mainly from Britain, the Mediterranean, Japan and South America. She argues that understanding the potential of the enclosed garden requires us to think of it as both a design and an experience.

As climate change becomes an increasingly important component of architectural planning, the enclosed garden, which can mediate so effectively between interior and exterior, provides opportunities for sustainable design and closer contact with the natural landscape. Study of the evolution of enclosed gardens, and the concepts they generate, is a highly effective means for students to learn about the design requirements of outdoor space proximal to the built environment.

Captured Landscape provides architectural design undergraduates, and practising architects, with a broad range of information and design possibilities. It will also appeal to landscape architects, horticulturalists and a wider audience of all those who are interested in garden design.

Kate Baker is an architect and has been a lecturer at the University of Portsmouth since 1992. Before that she was a principal in an architectural firm, with 15 years of experience in architectural practice, and taught part-time at the University of Cambridge. She is particularly interested in the relationship between architecture and landscape, and our sensory perception of space. Baker is an active researcher and has published a range of papers in these subject areas.

Captured Landscape

The paradox of the enclosed garden

Kate Baker

Routledge
Taylor & Francis Group

LONDON AND NEW YORK

First published 2012
by Routledge
2 Park Square, Milton Park, Abingdon, Oxon OX14 4RN

Simultaneously published in the USA and Canada
by Routledge
711 Third Avenue, New York, NY 10017

Routledge is an imprint of the Taylor & Francis Group, an informa business

British Library Cataloguing in Publication Data
A catalogue record for this book is available from the British Library

Library of Congress Cataloging in Publication Data
Baker, Kate, 1949–.
  Captured landscape: the paradox of the enclosed garden/Kate Baker.
  p. cm.
  Includes bibliographical references and index.
  1. Landscape design.   2. Gardens – Design.   I. Title.
  II. Title: Paradox of the enclosed garden.
  SB472.45.B35 2012
  712 – dc23   2011017022

ISBN: 978–0–415–56228–7 (hbk)
ISBN: 978–0–415–56229–4 (pbk)

Typeset in Univers
by Florence Production Ltd, Stoodleigh, Devon
Printed in Great Britain by Ashford Colour Press Ltd., Gosport, Hampshire

Contents

Preface   vii

Introduction   1

1   Defining the territory: the ambiguous nature of
an enclosed garden   5

2   From patio to park: the enclosed garden as a
generator of architectural and landscape design   35

3   Taming nature – and the way to Paradise   69

4   Ritual and emptiness – and the rigour of
developing an idea   103

5   Sensory seclusion: the affective garden,
the garden room as a scene for living   131

6   Detachment: the separation of the garden
from the building   159

Epilogue   187

Notes   189

Selected bibliography   195

Illustration credits   199

Index   205

Preface

Contact with the natural environment can be very compromised in the urban environment that most of us inhabit. We live and work indoors with only visual contact with the outside world, which can lead to misunderstanding and ignorance of the context of many places. In the following chapters I will examine sites where there has been a deliberate effort to negotiate the boundaries between the interior and exterior environment through the creation of an enclosed garden – by nature an ambiguous place – and demonstrate the possibilities of re-connecting with the natural world through its application to architectural and landscape design.

The book will start by asking what we mean by an enclosed garden, and what are its constituent parts? Why might it be significant, and how does it work? In the following chapters I will investigate a range of sizes and scales of buildings and gardens that use the basic idea or *typology* of the enclosed garden, to demonstrate its versatility of spatial arrangements for accommodating the needs of the users. I will go on to explore the origins of the enclosed garden, outline its deep history and discuss how it has flourished in specific periods. Three chapters that discuss different aspects of the enclosed garden will follow this, demonstrating certain design principles that are still relevant today. Chapter 4 'Ritual and emptiness' will look at the enclosed garden as a focal point that we use to orient our movements and give access to other spaces, and look at how its internal focus has embodied ideas. Chapter 5 'Sensory seclusion' explores the inhabited garden that we experience through our senses. Finally, Chapter 6 'Detachment' discusses gardens that are not directly connected to a building and have a particular purpose, that nevertheless embody architectural ambitions.

The book concentrates on examples of enclosed gardens from three main climatic zones: the hot dry desert conditions of the southern Mediterranean and the Middle East, the western and northern Mediterranean, and the more temperate climate of Europe further north. I will demonstrate how the same underlying type of enclosure can be adapted to suit a wide range of conditions and extremes of climate.

I will make use of an experiential description as an essential way of being able to convey the atmosphere that gives each garden its character and sense of place, which will be put alongside a more objective analysis. This is both a source book and a reference guide to good design. There are many examples taken from the past, but it is not seen as a critical history, and where historical examples have been used, only periods that have direct relevance to contemporary design issues are discussed.

My approach is deliberately cross-disciplinary in an attempt to bring out the interdependence of both architecture and landscape. Although it is mainly aimed at students of architectural and landscape design, I hope that it can reach a wider audience of people who are interested in this particular phenomenon of capturing the landscape, and converting it, through the architecture and architectural elements, into memorable places.

Many examples included are chosen for their success as habitable spaces as much as for their architectural merits. In some cases there has been no self-conscious designing of the space at all, but the spaces are important in that they have acquired a sense of place over time and human investment and can be used as precedents for good practice.

Acknowledgements

My thanks to:

Elizabeth McKellar for her detailed comments and proof reading, Peter Middleton for his comments and insight, particularly with the early drafts, Nick Timms for discussing the ideas that have come out of our joint projects with architecture diploma students over several years, and visiting many of the places mentioned, Mary Ann Steane also for discussing the ideas and visiting many of the places mentioned, Martin Pearce for his thoughts on the shape of the book, Mark West for drawing the plans and help with many software problems, also Khalid Saleh for his help with drawings, Anna Cady and Paul Clough for their support with the images and editorial advice, Lorraine Farrelly for her encouragement to write the book in the first place, the University of Portsmouth for its support in funding and providing time for writing and further funding for visiting some of the locations discussed, everyone, especially colleagues, who have kindly taken photographs for me, my family – Peter, George and Harriet – who have had to live with mess and anguish when things did not always go according to plan.

Introduction

The paradox of the enclosed garden

There is something perennially compelling about enclosed gardens. Since I was a student, they have captivated me with their intensity, their containment and the ambiguity of their nature whether old or new. Staking out, wrapping round and capturing the landscape has been expressed in different ways and in many cultures to provide us with many memorable architectural settings. As you walk around a stone-flagged cloister, for instance, the acoustic of the space makes the sound of our footsteps ring out as it bounces off the walls, and at the same time we are aware of the visual rhythm of the openings in the inner cloister wall as we pass them. We can smell the plants, feel the wind and still be sheltered from the weather and we are safe from the outside world. This outside unbound space might be the urban environment that sprawls around us and which most of us live in, or the open countryside. The enclosed garden is the mediator between dwelling and nature, building and landscape, and this is one of the keys to its longevity in the canon of architectural and landscape designs over many centuries.

What I hope to do in the following pages is to convey the important role these spaces have to play in architectural and landscape design. By looking at case studies, I will demonstrate the importance of the enclosure of outdoor space as a design principle. Throughout the discussion I have put much emphasis on an experiential approach, to counterbalance studies where abstract ideas analysis and history tend to be the dominant theme. I wish to test abstract against experience, and draw attention to an understanding of design through a sensuous embodied perception of a particular aspect of *place*.

Why is the enclosed garden such an enduring phenomenon? What makes it such a powerful form, and what relevance does it have to contemporary designs? The way architects incorporate buildings in a landscape is a statement of our cultural moment and our respect for the land and its resources. Industrialisation and urbanisation have been forcing our relationship with the land to the periphery of our lives, and there is a danger of losing touch with the natural world. Enclosing a space and transforming it into a garden brings us face to face with the natural world, providing the opportunity to observe and reflect upon it.

An enclosed garden is often called an outdoor room because of its similarity and complementary properties to what we comprehend as an internal room. The enclosed garden has also gained a reputation for being more than the sum of its parts. Although it could be nothing more than a sectioned-off parcel of land, there are many examples where the garden has developed into a space full of resonance. Its fundamental typology provides possibilities for a specific response to its location. We tend to think of architecture as a three-dimensional envelope, an object containing a sealed interior environment, and of landscape design as the shaping of the earth on which the building sits. This attitude has been at the expense of enclosure of the land, and encouraged architecture to avoid working effectively with the living landscape.

I have chosen some outstanding examples of enclosed gardens from across the history of architecture and garden design, and will analyse and discuss their appropriateness as templates for contemporary design. The risk of conventional analysis of enclosed gardens is that it will be based only on an act of seeing. To grasp why this may not be adequate, I want to reflect on the iconography of flowers and gardens in traditional Persian rug and carpet design. These carpets depict the layout of the garden, and elaborate on this theme in a manner that will help us go beyond purely visual approaches. The carpet in *Figure 0.1* shows an intricate classic Persian enclosed garden with a pattern of channels of water flowing from a central pool and dividing the garden into four, its flowering beauty a reminder during the winter of the gardens enjoyed in the summer months. In such traditional Islamic designs the garden layout always starts with a clear geometry. We have a sense of this planar geometry as we walk around an enclosed space, and are able to appreciate the whole as if we were able to see it from above. Now, If we look again at the carpet illustration in detail we see both the pattern and geometry from a bird's eye view, as a horizontal *plan*, the abstract of our idea of the room as enclosed by walls, floors and ceiling, and as part of a larger architectural building plan. But if we look closely at the carpet, we see also that some of the plants are depicted vertically in *elevation*. This may seem no more than the limitations of an art that has not developed perspective, but what is far more likely is that the artists wanted to evoke the way we might experience them as we walk through them. This experience of movement through the garden is, I think, crucial to understanding how the enclosed garden works.

We talk a lot about 'the view', going to far away places, tops of mountains and craggy coastlines to admire it – a limitless panorama set before our eyes. Housing design in the twentieth and twenty-first centuries has provided us with a version of this view. We have limitless glass openings, covering entire walls of buildings. We 'let the outside in' and can almost feel that we are outside, in nature, as we sit in our living rooms and with panoramic views in our workplaces, but at the same time we have

0.1
Persian Carpet 1670-1750, depicting an enclosed garden, bordered, with an interpretation of the four rivers dividing the garden into four distinct areas representing both the plan, the horizontal, and also the foliage in elevation, the vertical.

lost something. We are visually satisfied, but undergo a sensory deprivation of the external world. We can see everything at once, and there can be a lack of definition, and no surprises. We have lost the framed view. With our sealed units we have also lost the physical ambiguity between the outside and the inside, and how, say, a veranda can provide shade and comfort. We have lost the sense of enclosure that buildings and building components can give us. They can create interior external spaces and become an outdoor room – an extension of the house. We have wanted to look outward, in favour of any sense we might need for interiority and reflection. Capturing landscape again gives us the opportunity to inwardly gaze and reflect on the broader landscapes of our lives.

1 Defining the territory

The ambiguous nature of an enclosed garden

Discovery

It's the beginning of June, and my friend and I have come, by recom-
mendation, to visit the gardens of the Mottisfont Abbey[1] in Hampshire, UK.
After looking around the building we walk away, past the old stable block,
into the grounds. So far, nothing appears striking enough to justify the
garden's reputation.

We arrive at a closed-off section of the garden and see a small neatly
shaped opening in a hedge beside a high wall. This gives no clue to what
might be in store, apart from a faint waft of scent in the air caught in a
coolish breeze. We walk on through a confined space lined with hedges
and a wall high enough to cut off any direct view. There is no apparent exit.
As we walk down the space we see a pool of light on the ground, and an
opening appears to the left. We walk through it into a large self-contained
courtyard, with people milling about, queuing for ice creams, choosing plants
to buy, looking at a small exhibition, or sitting down with cups of tea around
a group of outdoor tables. Conversation fills the air. This is a courtyard large
enough to support a series of activities – the visiting members of the public
as well as the gardeners who tend the grounds – yet small enough for us
to feel the sense of containment that the walls provide. Beyond the crowds
we see another small opening in the far wall with light streaming through
that catches our eyes and we are drawn towards it. The journey continues
and we pass through the wall, into paradise.

Pinks, irises, lilies, foxgloves, peonies, lilies, salvia, geraniums and
many other plants surround us, all in full bloom, dispersed among one of

Britain's national collections of old roses. A cloud of scents envelopes us as we walk in. The intensity is overwhelming. Our senses are seduced and we are immersed in the experience of the enclosed garden.

The garden invites us to walk along a straight path toward the centre, toward the sound and movement of a constant trickle of water from a pool. A never-ending variety of colour combinations, texture, scent and shape encourage us to explore. We can disperse and be lost in among the drifts of herbaceous plants, sit on a bench in a shady corner, or find a patch of lawn to sit on.

We start to be aware of what is creating this experience, a dialogue between the architectural and garden components. The garden is divided into two interconnecting areas by high brick walls on all sides. Each has a central focal point that helps us negotiate our way around. Paths are placed strategically and the sparse openings in the walls provide 'windows' that provide us with distinct framed views.

An experience like this is a reminder that to understand such gardens, it would not be enough to think of them by only looking diagrammatically, by reading the 'plan', or even as visual phenomena to be observed only. They demand an active involvement by the participant. What they *are* is an immersive *experience*, just as a play or concert is the *performance*, and not the written script or score.

Exploring the idea

Captured landscape is as much an idea as a reality. By internalising landscape within boundary walls, we transform it, and thereby demonstrate our beliefs and attitudes toward nature.[2] Creating a boundary wall around a piece of land enables us to comprehend it as a defined and owned space. The construction of an enclosing wall also has material consequences, making it possible to control or alter many features of the interior, including the climate. In Figures 1.1, 1.2 and 1.3 the act of making a boundary around a plot of land in three very different locations gives each space a distinct definition. *Figure 1.1* is in the Netherlands, where the owner has staked out a place in the dunes; *Figure 1.2* is on the Isle of Wight in the UK, where the house owner has a defined territory within a sea of wheat; *Figure 1.3* is in the south of France, where a church has claimed space around it in an undefined landscape. In each, the interior space, an enclosed garden, is as necessary to the character of the dwelling place as its internal architecture and its outward façades. By manipulating the enclosed landscape, keeping

1.1
Fisherman's allotment in
the dunes with vegetable
plots, with boundary
clearly marked out.
Wimmenummer Duinen,
Egmond aan Zee, North
Holland.

1.2
House and garden
surrounded by a sea of
wheat in the Isle of Wight,
UK.

1.3
Church and graveyard
protected by wall in open
countryside, Les Alpilles,
France.

untamed nature at bay, we actually intensify our relationship with nature, whether our purpose is for cultivation or enjoyment, for our bodies or our souls. In many cases this can be described as a poetic act. Some of the most memorable places around the globe are those where architecture, architectural components and landscape collude and affect our sensibilities.

1.4
Limits to limited space.

Is it an interior space with no ceiling or is it a garden that has the properties of an indoor room? An enclosed garden is neither and both, an ambiguous space by its very nature. Because our eyes are not free to travel to the horizon when we are within them, unlike other garden spaces, its scale can have the familiarity and even the security of a room, particularly within an architectural context. The view is interrupted by a horizontal plane that continually brings our focus back into the space, visually separating us from what lies beyond it. The enclosed garden gives limits to limitless space. *Figures 1.4, 1.5, 1.6.*

1.5
Restricted views.

The term *outdoor room* is well known in the realm of landscape and garden design, whereas in architectural design the relationship between interior and exterior space since the early twentieth century, particularly in the West, has tended to have more emphasis on a *visual* connection between the two. However, there is a lineage of enclosed gardens described as outdoor rooms that can be traced back throughout the history of garden design, and has continued into the twentieth and twenty-first centuries. For example, a series of outdoor rooms have been devised at Hidcote Manor,[3] originally to protect tender plants on an exposed site. It became one of the most influential gardens of its time. Hedges maintained with architectural precision enclose the Red Borders garden. They give it shape in winter months, and provide a backing in summer for the rich vibrant crimsons and oranges of its herbaceous plants. *Figure 1.7.*

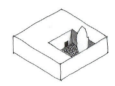

1.6
Room in a building.

1.7
Hidcote Manor, UK. Hedges act as walls to the Red Borders garden, making an architectural statement together with two symmetrically placed pavilions. The orderly rows of severely cut, pleached hornbeams complete the enclosure at a higher level, and provide us with a visual connection to the next 'room', and a restricted view of the land beyond it.

1.8
An enclosed garden in
Cordoba is used for a
business meeting in the
morning when it is still
shaded and pleasantly
cool.

Wherever the location, outdoor rooms create spaces distinct from their surroundings, whether they are adjacent to buildings, within the cityscape, or the open countryside. They can make a contribution to our daily lives, such as providing extensions to living areas and increasing the usable space of a dwelling. The patio garden in southern Spain where the climate invites outdoor living exemplifies how such spaces can be integral to the functioning of the building. *Figure 1.8.*

Characteristics and component parts

The whole question of the relation of vegetation to architecture is a very large one and to know what to place where, when to stop, and when to abstain altogether, requires knowledge on both sides. The horticulturalist generally errs in putting his plants and shrubs and climbers everywhere, and in not even discriminating between the relative fitness of any two plants whose respective right use may be quite different and perhaps antagonistic. The architect, on the other hand, is often wanting in sympathy with beautiful vegetation. The truth appears to be that for the best building and planting, where both these crafts must meet and overlap and work together, the architect and gardener must have some knowledge of each others business.

Gertrude Jekyll, *Wall and Water
Gardens*, 2005

When we consider a room we think of an internal space with walls, floors and ceiling, and with at least one entry point, the door, and an opening to allow light in and to look out. We will furnish it with things appropriate to its use. A domestic room may well have a carpet; the walls will have a finished surface and most likely will be hung with pictures. It will have means of controlling the environmental conditions through varying its heating, lighting and ventilation. Rooms provide security, privacy, safety and confinement, places where we are removed and distant from the world at large. Enclosed gardens provide these conditions as well, but where nature is brought in alongside the man-made, climate and ground conditions are utilised, and where the ceiling is the sky. The success of captured landscape lies in first, the treatment of the ground – the paving and planting, and second, in the treatment of its boundary walls. *Figure 1.9.*

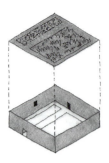

1.9
Vertical and horizontal components.

The horizontal plane – the ground

In an outdoor room, the floor connects us directly with the structure of the earth, and with nature. It grounds us and is a reminder of the frailty of living things. Although the garden is subject to specific soil and weather conditions, and needs to be tended, enclosure can reduce potentially harmful external influences, and planting can flourish. The floor covering is not necessarily all planting, however. Courtyards around the Mediterranean and the Middle East, where water is scarce, are predominantly paved. *Figure 1.10.* Planting will be inserted within a covering of paving, or placed in pots. *Figure 1.11.* Contact with plants, however minimal, is highly valued in areas where the land is parched. Water, the source of life, is a recurring theme, and expressions of its importance are evident through the depth of historical examples and breadth of cultural variation and invention. Flowerbeds in Islamic gardens at the height of the Islamic empire were sometimes sunk

1.10
Looking down on a courtyard in the Alhambra. The paving, simply made from two different coloured pebbles, is as patterned as if it were a carpet.

1.11
Courtyard garden showing small amount of earth for plants to reduce water loss through evaporation. Riad el Qadi, Marrakech, Morocco.

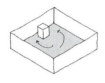

1.12
There is adequate space around the pavilion for it not to dominate the enclosure.

below ground so that when the plants had grown, the flowers would be at ground level, giving the appearance of a flat carpet. This had practical as well as aesthetic value as there is considerably less water loss if only the tops of the plants are exposed to direct sunlight.

Enclosed gardens may also contain rooms within them, perhaps in the form of a pavilion. *Figure 1.12.* These are likely to be considerably smaller than their surroundings, and thus will not fight with the integrity of the overall space. Wash-houses in monasteries *Figure 1.13* or kiosks of the large Islamic gardens *Figure 1.14* will be secondary in scale to the spaces themselves, the equivalent of aedicular structures within architectural interiors, or even pieces of furniture.

1.13
The wash-house of a Cistercian monastery sits within the intimate space of the cloister garden without dominating it.

The vertical plane – the boundary wall

The wall is the major component that shapes an enclosed garden and gives it much of its character. Although we usually associate walls with solid materials such as stone or brick, walls can also be created by hedges or a row of trees. A well-managed hedge provides shelter and security, a habitat for wildlife, and provides a more direct relationship with the natural world than an inanimate material. We can cut and shape hedging with precision to give an even planar surface. Different types of walling can be combined in one space. The garden in *Figure 1.15* illustrates four alternative ways of providing enclosure. The building itself provides a solid side of rendered

1.15
The Machuca Patio in the Alhambra, Granada, Spain, illustrates four different ways of bounding space and enclosing a garden/courtyard, using both hedge and building.

brickwork, with views into the garden from ground and first-floor level. There is a colonnade to one side of it, to walk along. Opposite the building there is a solid hedge cutting off the view beyond, and turning our gaze inward, and on the fourth side the hedge has a series of openings cut in a rhythmical pattern that responds to the colonnade opposite. This open hedge mediates between inside and out.

Hole in the wall

Entrances and exits are often played down in enclosed gardens, which tend to have very few other openings. From outside, a view into the enclosure may well arouse curiosity, and encourage us to search for a hidden entrance. From within, a restricted view can also arouse our curiosity of another place beyond the sheltering wall of the enclosure.

A glimpse of bright light through a small opening in the walled garden at Tresco Abbey Gardens, Isles of Scilly, UK, is enough to entice us. *Figure 1.16.* The outer wall of the garden to Mesquite in Cordoba, Spain, has openings that give us a preview of what we will experience if we enter. *Figure 1.17.*

1.16
The bright light and restricted view through the door at the Abbey Gardens, Tresco, UK, gives the the suggestion of something to be discovered on the other side . . .

1.17
The garden courtyard to the Mesquite in Cordoba, Spain, can be seen through a few openings in its boundary wall.

Where there is a series of connected spaces, openings give clues to the journey's destination. Within the monastery at Santi Quatro Coronatti in Rome, the rhythm of the changing light quality can be seen as your gaze is drawn through layers of open spaces framed by the architecture, creating an atmosphere of calm as well as a sense of separation from the city. The inner and most private cloister is deep within the plan and has no obvious way in or out, quite separate from any direct link. *Figures 1.18, 1.19, 1.20.*

1.18
The severe high walls at Santi Quatro Coronatti, Rome, give a sense of enclosure, even imprisonment, but the sunlight falling on them and the alternating pattern of light and dark between building and courtyard is very striking, and entices you through the spaces.

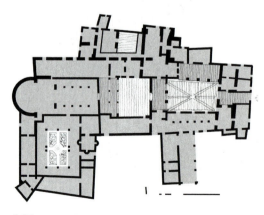

1.19
Santi Quatro Coronatti, Rome, ground floor plan indicating processional route to the church and private inner cloister.

1.20
Simplified plan of Santi Quatro Coronatti, Rome, showing proportion and juxtaposition of internal and external spaces.

Defining the territory

The porous wall

The boundaries of enclosed gardens can be designed to have *layers* of enclosure, habitable porous zones that mediate between interior and exterior conditions. They are the parts of the building, usually at ground level, that we have close physical contact with, where scale, proportion and choice of materials are important. The colonnade or cloister is widely used, and is a very versatile space, its purpose varying according to the use of the building and the prevailing climatic conditions, and it is usually the main circulation area around an enclosed garden. *Figure 1.21*. It allows natural light to penetrate deep into a building interior, while preventing the full intrusion of direct sunlight. In many situations it provides shelter where complete exposure to the climate would not always be tolerable. A colonnade acts as a threshold area, preparing us for either the interior or the exterior, to expand or contract into, or just to walk in. *Figures 1.22, 1.23*. The boundary wall can also be a site for people to make use of. The sides to one of the gardens at the University of Lusiada, in Lisbon, Portugal, are inhabited along its length and take on a life of their own. The façades open up and become animated, encouraging innovative use. *Figure 1.24*.

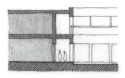

1.21
Section through a colonnaded building.

1.22
A perimeter walkway at the Catholic University of Santiago, Chile, connecting enclosure and building.

Containment – the sense of the garden as a whole

> The enclosure not only establishes a specific relationship with a specific place but is the principle by which a human group states its very relationship with nature and the cosmos. In addition, the enclosure is the form of the thing; how it presents itself to the outside world; how it reveals itself.[4]
>
> Vittorio Giegotti, 1979

The enclosed garden is a tangible space. Through providing us with a sense of containment it responds to both the imaginative and practical sides of our natures. It invites us to see it as metaphorical space and project ideas onto it, as well as a place to dwell in or for nurturing plants. *Figure 1.25.*

1.25
Containers of events, ideas and plants.

Of people – places to dwell in

Enclosed gardens – outdoor rooms – are, by implication, gathering places. In practical terms they enable us to orient ourselves in relation to a building. They also give us access to the natural world in a controlled manner. Within a private house they can be additional living spaces, and within larger institutional buildings, enclosed gardens can absorb many people, providing conditions for circulating in and around the building complex, or be temporarily transformed into social spaces for gatherings and other events. At an urban scale, gardens are often referred to as the green lungs of the city, vitally essential to its health, and an overspill for city dwellers to escape to.

Whether they are domestic, institutional or urban, well-designed enclosed spaces have a scale to fit their purpose and surroundings. They invite participation; the privacy and small scale of the domestic setting such as the enclosed garden in *Figure 1.26* where the house and wall create a sheltered secure area outside the house, the more formal surroundings of the institution or the company of strangers and private intimacy within a very public space. *Figure 1.27.*

1.26
Relaxing in early summer at Manor Farm, the outdoor space is enclosed partly by the house, and partly through an enclosing wall that protects it on a windswept hillside. Architect: Tod Wakefield Architects.

1.27
The Embankment garden in London comes alive with people on a sunny day in early summer; in one of the busiest parts of London. Its boundaries are the backs of high-rise buildings of the Strand and Charing Cross Station. A thicket of trees and shrubs protects you from the busy road along the Embankment.

Of ideas – metaphorical space, the representation of beliefs

Enclosed gardens provide us with a space to celebrate and contemplate the human condition, and can be an embodiment of a philosophy of life. They can be seen as condensed versions of nature, containing the essence of the world and the relationship of all things.[5] At certain historical moments, the art of the garden has achieved the high status of great religious art. This is evidenced in Islamic secular gardens that represent Earthly Paradise. *Figure 1.28.* The cloisters in Christian monastic communities can be seen as references to the Garden of Eden where they were used as a conduit and aid to prayer and meditation. *Figure 1.29.* Enclosed gardens can be entirely symbolic, and are expressed through geometry alone. The highly decorated courtyards adjoining Islamic religious buildings, for example, will usually contain water but have no planting at all. Chinese and Japanese gardens originate in Buddhist ideals of spiritual harmony where the nature of reality and existence can be contemplated through observance of mimetic representation of natural forms. In the great Buddhist gardens of China, stones and rocks play a significant part in garden design; they can, for instance, be chosen so that their shapes and positioning evoke, in miniature, the misty mountain ranges of the wild landscape. In the dry gardens of Japan, gravel is frequently used to imitate water, suggesting a 'sea' between rocks that become 'islands'.

Defining the territory

1.28
Amber Palace, Jaipur, India. The secular garden is rich with foilage, but planting is kept to a regular geometric pattern of beds. A variation of the Islamic paradise garden has been used for its design, with a central pool, four fountains, and four paths leading onto a central small podium.

1.29
The cloister at Avignon Cathedral, France.

Of utility – for the production and observation of plants

Enclosed gardens can be very functional places, particularly for horticulture. The enclosure can prolong planting seasons, and allow for the propagation of plants that under normal circumstances would be too tender to grow in that location. The boundary wall protects the interior from unwanted predators, so plants can be nurtured without the risk of animals damaging or eating them. They lend themselves not just to horticulture, but also to scientific experiment, and education. The carpet of the outdoor room becomes a surface for close observation.

Response to climate

The inclusion of an enclosed garden in a design, whether it is landscape or architectural, increases the possibility of manipulating the existing environment. *Figure 1.30*. It acts as a climate control 'chamber'. Solid walls on all sides give the opportunity to exploit both sun and shade throughout the day. They break the prevailing wind and provide shelter for tender plants, and during daylight hours, particularly if they are built of a heavy load-bearing material such as brick, stone or concrete, they absorb the warmth of the sun. In turn they will radiate heat back out into the space at night. This can be advantageous for plants whose natural habitat is from a warmer climate. In hot climates an enclosed garden can make living conditions tolerable, and in more temperate climates people will be able to sit outside for considerably longer in the evening before having to retreat indoors, particularly if they are in the lee of a wall that has been soaked by the sun throughout the day. The net effect is that the enclosure provides a more stable ambient climate than its exterior surroundings.

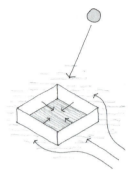

1.30
Environmental control.

Enclosed gardens evolved in climates with long hot dry seasons, where protection from sun and wind has been a necessity. This has given rise to much inventiveness by harnessing local conditions through simple means, such as orientation, proportioning of the space to provide shade, creating air movement and humidification. These are achieved by adjusting the size and type of building components, or plants, or a combination of the two. Enclosed gardens can be tuned to seasonal variation, through the permanent structure of the building, through adjustments to the boundary wall, and through planting.

Sun and shade

The inclusion of a square enclosed garden oriented toward the four cardinal points can maximise solar gain throughout the day and the season. This is necessary in cooler climates to create warmth, rather than nearer the tropics where the aim is to keep the sun out of living areas as much as possible. Some of the clearest examples can be found where the climate is harsh, and living and growing conditions necessitate adaptation and respect for the climate for survival, both for people and for plants. Many innovations have been developed in vernacular housing within the hot and arid zones of the Middle East, North Africa and the Indian subcontinent. By creating small internal open courtyards to buildings, with high walls, much of the space can be shaded throughout the day, keeping off the direct radiant heat from the sun. This type of courtyard has developed widely, with many local variations. *Figures 1.31, 1.32.*

Seasonal adaptations have been devised, such as the use of fabric. Canvas sails, curtains across the sky, are much used when the sun is overhead, and can easily be spanned securely between walls of deep courtyards to increase the shade. The small courtyards of southern Spain

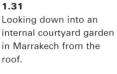

1.31
Looking down into an internal courtyard garden in Marrakech from the roof.

1.32
Section through the house, based on Dar el Qadi, Marrakech, where the shared access alleyway is tunnelled through on the right.

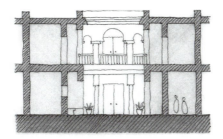

1.33
Cordoba, Spain. Canvas sails are suspended over narrow courtyards. The heat of
the sun causes the warmed air to rise to the underside of the sail, creating draughts
of cooler air through the galleries and the entrance hallway. These simple methods
of climate control can be seen both in Roman and Islamic traditions, and are still
very effective today.

have given rise to inventive ways of creating shade. *Figure 1.33* shows a
simple flexible device, using only sail cloth, rope and pulleys, that shields
the sun when it is overhead in the summer months. As it is not tightly fitted
it has a further advantage of letting the space *breathe.*

Air movement

Enclosure implies a lack of air movement. This can be both a help and a
hindrance. Cutting out the prevailing winds on an exposed site can create
growing conditions that would be impossible in the open countryside,
particularly in temperate climates. In hot climates, creating air movement
within enclosed gardens can be essential to make living conditions bearable.
Devices have evolved to create air movement in a way that provides
locations within a dwelling that can take advantage of a cooling flow of air.

In the courtyard houses of the Maghreb,[6] after the temperature has
dropped at night the warm air rises and is replaced by cooler air. This
accumulates and seeps into the surrounding rooms.[7] The air remains cool
in the morning as the courtyard or garden will be shaded by the building.
As the day wears on, the warmest air will not enter the inner space, but
eddy around the building, leaving the interior considerably cooler and more
pleasant than the outside. The building and surrounding wall also protect

the space from any hot dry winds. This system has been refined over time and an even more efficient method has evolved with the use of a double courtyard. Two open spaces are designed into a single dwelling. A semi-enclosed loggia-type space, a *takhtabush,* is created between them. It will look into the inner shaded courtyard, and have a screen separating it from the larger garden. The breeze is drawn through from the cooler to the hotter space.[8] *Figure 1.34* shows an adapted version in a house in Cairo. The *takhtabush* lies midway between the two courtyards, allowing the air to be pulled through between them, thus providing a pleasantly cool place to sit and socialise.

Water and humidity

Enclosed gardens, unless they are designed to be plant-less, cannot survive without water. They depend on its availability, either on site or through the ingenuity and resourcefulness of the garden owners and their capacity to obtain and store water. Scarcity has given water great value and significance, particularly in hot climates. Our appreciation of oases – verdant areas in the desert – thrives on the contrast between heat and dust and the shady planting made possible by the presence of water. In cooler climates it has still been revered, more through its symbolic significance than of necessity. Enclosed gardens can provide natural air conditioning, with several methods of humidifying. Water in the form of a fountain or pool will give off water vapour that, mixed with air, will increase the humidity.[9] In hot climates large bowls of water are often to be found in

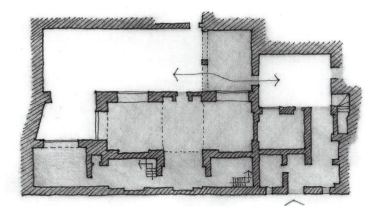

1.34
Plan of the As-Suhaymi house at Al-Asfār, Cairo, showing circulation of air between the two courtyards through the *takhtabush.*

courtyards, where the water is left to evaporate. Plants also play a vital role, by providing water vapour, which expires through their leaves. An enclosure sealed off by walls plays a large part in retaining the moisture levels, preventing humidified air being blown away. A canopy of trees also makes a contribution by slowing down upward evaporation.

Water, shade and planting

As well as looking pleasing, enclosed gardens, through the use of the plants, create more comfortable conditions for human habitation than open courtyards. Water is essential to keep the plants alive and when it is scarce it needs to be looked after with care and used sparingly. This can be seen in many examples in countries around the Mediterranean through integrating building, planting and water. The Court of the Oranges, in front of the Mesquite,[10] in Cordoba in southern Spain, now a World Heritage site, owes much to the ingenuity of its original designers and their plans to conserve water. The roof of the mosque provides a very large surface area with the potential to collect rainwater. As there are long periods of drought, and water is a precious commodity, chutes were designed to collect rainwater run-off, and store it underground. [11]

This reservoir provided water for the two fountains for the necessary ritual ablutions to take place before entering the mosque for prayer, and we can assume that it was also used for irrigation. The courtyard is large, and filled with orange, cypress and palm trees that make a canopy over the whole of the area, providing shade for visitors. As they are evergreens, there is continuous shade throughout the year. Today, a series of channels distributes the water that connects to encircling 'pools' around each tree. *Figure 1.35.*

1.35
Water is channelled into the pools around the trees when they are irrigated.

These, together with the intricately laid paving, contribute to the decorative pattern and harmony of the surface of this fine and unique open space. [12]

Although there is no evidence to support the design of the yard as an echo of the interior, if we look at the space through twenty-first century eyes, the regular grid of the trees gives us a sense of continuity of the design between exterior and interior, with the pattern of the trees reciprocating the continuous gridded pattern of columns and arches.[13] The arches in the façade of the building that surrounds the Court would originally have been open, making more of a visual connection between interior and exterior. We can also read the Court indirectly as representing the forest, a canopy provided by nature, Paradise and the Garden of Eden.[14] *Figures 1.36, 1.37, 1.38.*

1.36
Inside the Mesquite, showing the gridded pattern of columns.

1.37
Mesquite, Court of Oranges, Cordoba, showing the gridded pattern of planting.

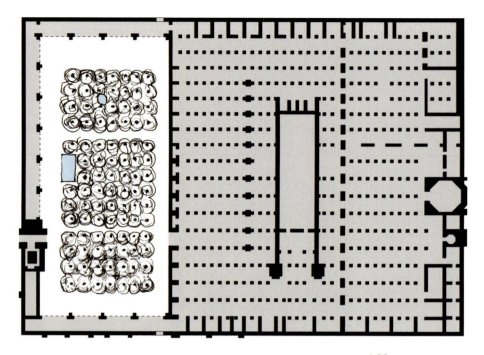

1.38
Ground floor plan of the
Mesquite, Cordoba,
showing the grids of both
the planting and the
columns within the
buildings.

Aspect and temperature

Capturing and enclosing a patch of land allows for adaptation of existing
conditions to take advantage of aspect and temperature variation. It has
particularly played an important part with the establishment of new
communities in Europe. The planning of a monastery, for example, took
weather conditions into consideration. The cloister was placed on the south
side of the church and was much shorter in height, and so it was never in
the church's shadow, guaranteeing the greatest amount of sunlight available
to fall onto it. Its total enclosure ensured the lessening of cold winds, and
the cloister itself provided a sheltered covered space for carrying out daily
duties and rituals.

Enclosure has been the starting point of creating specialised spaces
– orchards, kitchen gardens and herbariums, providing food for the
community, and medicines for the sick. The earliest known planning of these
specialised spaces is at the monastery of St Gall in Switzerland. *Figure 1.39*.
It was drawn up in the ninth century and shows us a series of gardens that
were needed for the community to survive. Although these plans were
never followed completely, they represent a pattern of life for a community
that relied on small enclosed spaces allocated for particular activities.

Specialisation has continued, particularly for horticulture. Botanic
gardens placed within enclosing walls, for example, flourished from the
sixteenth century onwards. The walled kitchen gardens of large country
houses in Britain were very popular in the eighteenth and nineteenth

1.39
Plan of the monastery at St Gall, showing proposed layouts of enclosures.

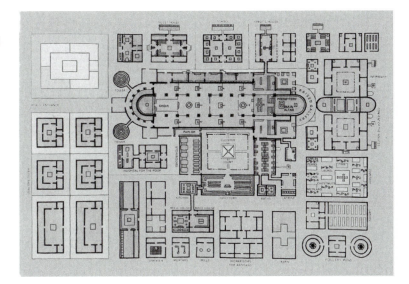

centuries. They were repositories for exotic plants collected from all over the world, later to be displayed or feasted on by the owners.

Response to site

Adaptation of natural landscapes

Every site destined for an architectural or garden project is unique. Taking account of existing conditions is a given and will contribute toward its *genius loci,* its sense of place. As we can see from St. Gall, enclosure can be a starting point for the organisation of spaces. Creating external rooms is a way of working with the landscape. If a building site appears to be an awkward shape, or has a variety of levels within it, a central open space can provide a datum around which the differences of level can be reconciled.

Landscape/architecture/garden

One of the most spectacular examples of working closely with the land is the Generalife Gardens to the east of the Alhambra complex in Granada, Spain. Landscape is integrated with gardens and architecture, nature and artifice working together to near perfection. *Figure 1.40.* The gardens were originated in the fourteenth century as pleasure gardens on an adjacent hillside to the already existing and well-established Nazrid Palaces, and have developed and spread back along the hillside ever since.

There are three main components: the original pavilions with their patios, the formal 'New Gardens' and the Arena. The land has been

1.40
View of the Generalife from the Alhambra, looking across to the garden, terracing and pavilions.

manipulated through levelling and terracing, using a pallet of architecture, walls, hedges, individual trees and planting. Gardens have been created where their layouts have been tailored to fit the natural curve and slope of the hillside, adding drama to the already spectacular promontory.[15] The design of the individual spaces is formal and orthogonal throughout, but the experience of it is of three-dimensionally weaving through them as you step around and along the hillside. *Figure 1.41*.

The New Gardens comprise a formal linear sequence of outdoor rooms that sit on wide horizontal terracing built up with a sturdy stone retaining wall. They are enclosed with high cypress hedges that alternately deny and reveal the view.[16] Narrower terraces are cut on the lower sheltered western side that were originally used for growing produce for the Alhambra households. A shift of axis occurs at the end of the gardens to accommodate the pavilions that fit the increased curve of the hill, and command the best view. Even more dramatic is the ensemble of spaces and viewpoints of the original pavilions that have been worked into the hillside. For example, as you enter, you are drawn in through two courtyards. The first is mono-chromatic, cool and sunless, where nature is denied and the only view out is upwards. You climb a few steps, accommodating a natural level change into the next small patio, the Pole Patio, contained but sunlit, and finished

1.41
Bird's eye view of the
Generalife indicating the
detailed division of spaces
and level changes.

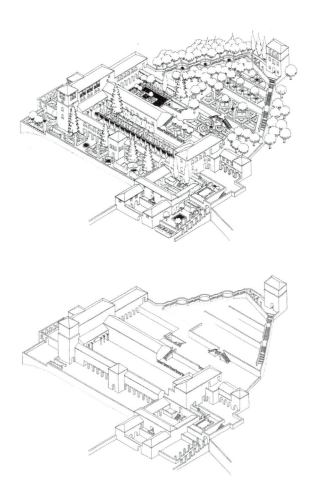

with decorative tiles and planted with orange trees; and then up more steps into the interior of the South Pavilion. Only when you are inside, and turn around, is the Patio Acequia revealed, a set piece of garden theatre, with no clear definition of where architecture stops and garden begins. It is a formal rectilinear space but with each side adjusted to the underlying landscape. To the east the boundary wall has no view out, but to the west there is a colonnaded walkway. A mirador (look-out) punctuates it, for you to pause and look back across to the palaces. There is another mirador at the far end, under the North Pavilion. Only at this point, through an arched opening, can you appreciate the height of the promontory above the town, and admire a sweeping panorama across Granada to the unpredictable and wilder landscape in the distance. You turn 180 degrees and look back onto the garden through a layered space, defined by two rows of columns, where nature is tamed and controlled. By continuing through the building you emerge into another more intimate garden, the Patio del Ciprés de la

1.42
Looking into the Patio
Sultana, a levelled
enclosed terrace
surrounded by solid walls
on three sides and a
'porous wall' of the North
Pavilion, that lets in the
breeze, and views out.

Sultana. *Figure 1.42*. The journey continues up into more terraces, giving
views down into the patios where the symmetrical organisation of planting,
water and architecture can be seen as a whole.

Adaptation of used landscapes

It is not unusual to reuse a site of occupation. Each era will take advantage
of what has preceded it, and it will be an expression of the values of that
period. The palimpsest of Rome exemplifies such continuity of use. Since
the late twentieth century we have necessarily become preoccupied with
the residue of a more recent past. Large industrial sites, originally located
outside towns in the nineteenth century, have now been encircled by the
suburbs, and rendered unsuitable for their purpose. There is a growing
number of these disused industrial landscapes, particularly in Europe, that
are being converted to create parks of our time, making use of their history
to create radical new designs that include new interpretations of enclosed
gardens.

New life for old sites

London's old docklands, where trading thrived in the nineteenth century,
are being reclaimed, after long periods of dereliction. Part of the strategy
has been to create a new park that reconnects the City to the river. A former
petrochemical site was levelled, covered and sealed[17] to form the new

Thames Barrier Park.[18] It has been transformed into a green 'plateau' that stretches out beside the Thames, its eastern boundary in line with the shimmering sculptural forms of the Thames Barrier.[19] A long strip has been cut out of the middle of the green horizontal plain, a deep channel designed to evoke the memory of the original Royal Docks, almost cutting the park in two. It has been transformed into an enclosed garden, a sheltered space hidden away from the windswept upper level. *Figure 1.43*. It starts and ends with water. At one end it butts up to the road, car park and station, with a piazza filled with bubbling fountains splashing onto the stone flags. At the other end, it ramps up to a small pavilion overlooking the Thames and the barrier itself, commemorating civilian victims of war from this part of London. The planting forms 'waves' of undulating hedges, giving a sense of movement and energy, and perhaps the memory of the water that once filled the dock. It has been described as 'the Green Dock, a ghost of its predecessor'.[20] Two bridges connect each side of the park.

Once you are inside the dock the atmosphere changes. The experience is of confinement and close proximity, which can induce a sense of claustrophobia in the faint-hearted. High battered walls covered with boxleaf honeysuckle block out the horizon on two sides. The pictorial pattern-making seen from above has been lost. You are given no choice but to follow the narrow paths. The planting is dense and you can enjoy the difference between this and the expansiveness of the windswept park. As you move along, the strips, colour, texture, shape and scent constantly change. The rises and falls of the wavy hedges provide changing views

1.43
Thames Barrier Park, London. Looking down into the sunken garden.

across the width of the garden. You could imagine it as a musical score. As you walk you beat out the rhythm of your stride in step with the undulations of the yew hedges and your experience of the garden with its artful planting and shaping, makes the music.

Reclamation and the ruin

Duisburg-Nord Landscape Park has been created in part of an old industrial area within the Ruhr Valley in Germany. It has been skilfully designed by Peter Latz and Partners, starting in 1991, into a complex continuum of spaces that acknowledges the industrial waste, decay and dereliction. It has been transformed into a park with many amenities for the large population that now surrounds it, and the site has been given a new life and a new meaning. The ruins have been kept and can now be appreciated for what they are, and to evoke memories of another era. At Duisburg we see an updated understanding of the romance of the ruin. The dialogue between nature and industrial decay can be seen as a healing process. The hope is that the land, over time, will become unpolluted as nature intervenes. The structures, often monumental in scale, will return to the earth.

Peter Latz has had no illusions about designing a park with any residual nineteenth-century ideals of romanticising the countryside or of the ruin only representing a glorious past. He is gravely concerned with reversing the damage done by the industrialists of the nineteenth and early twentieth centuries by converting and reclaiming the waste they left behind on the sites of their capital ventures. He has done this by transformation, accepting the past instead of concealing and covering over the cracks by hiding or removing the evidence: 'the vision for the new landscape should seek its justification exactly within the existing forms of demolition and exhaustion'. [21] Whereas much of the damage has been sealed up in the Thames Barrier Park, at Duisburg-Nord Landscape Park we are able to confront and reflect on the ruin.

The existing structure left by the industrial processing has been exploited to provide a network of high-level walkways, mainly constructed from recycled materials, to complement those on the ground. The height helps visitors orient themselves over the many hectares, enabling them to look down on a series of spaces, many of which have a certain grandeur. Their character comes directly from the surrounding weather-worn steel and concrete. Some, however, are discrete and have become intimate spaces within the wilderness of the park. There is a series of bunkers near the blast furnace that have been converted into small enclosed gardens. They can be looked at from the overhead catwalks, but are barely visible until you are almost on top of them. *Figure 1.44.* The existing rough concrete

1.44
Duisburg-Nord Landscape Park, Germany. View of one of the bunker gardens, with a catwalk behind it, and part of the monumental industrial ruins in the distance.

bunker walls have been left exposed. New doorways have been cut through to provide access. The marks of those who made them are left exposed around the threshold. *Figure 1.45*. The heaps of ore and coal deposits that used to be housed in them have been cleared and given way to plants. Evergreen strips of box hedge ripple across the enclosure, interspersed with deciduous flowering shrubs, providing seasonal change.

Nature has started to interact with the walls since the gardens were first planted, and now that these secret gardens have matured they have a magical quality that is only enhanced with the knowledge of their unprepossessing history. The scale of the site is reduced, providing a moment to pause as you cross the park; the bunkers are some of several havens, secret gardens within the vastness of the park that contribute to its success.

1.45
New doorway cut into the bunker garden.

The enclosed garden can be considered as a particular *type* of outdoor space, but within that type there can be a wide range of interpretations. Its ambiguity lends itself to interpretation by both the designers and the users, who can exploit its characteristics to suit their needs, both on the ground and surrounding boundaries. Where architecture is involved, an enclosed garden is important in being able to mediate between the interior and exterior. Its walls offer us a sense of enclosure that makes a space feel distinct from any other outside spaces. Its potential for adapting to the weather makes it useful in a wide range of climatic conditions. It lends itself to working with a particular site through the simplicity of its basic structure.

2 From patio to park

The enclosed garden as a generator of architectural and landscape design

The success of enclosed gardens lies in how they have been embedded in their surroundings; how the principles involved in including garden space contribute to the overall design. The methods of *carving out* or *wrapping* around a space in the centre of a building or landscape are simple and spatially economical devices for architectural design. The garden provides a focus and a unifying component for disparate parts of a building complex. It has similar properties to a courtyard, but the garden, by introducing nature and landscape, adds another dimension. This chapter will investigate the versatility of the plan and how the *footprint* of an enclosed garden can influence architectural designs, regardless of their size and dimensions, whether it is at the scale of an individual dwelling, a large building complex, or a public garden in a city. *Figures 2.1, 2.2.*

2.1
Inward looking, with central garden.

2.2
Circulation.

Small

The principle of garden as outdoor room is clear in small buildings such as the house, as the scale of exterior spaces is likely to relate to the rooms within it. The examples chosen in this section are all twentieth- and twenty-first-century buildings where the notion of enclosure has been explored and exploited in the design. In all of them there is a dialogue between the inner and the outer. The quality of the spaces relies on the reciprocity between architecture and garden creating a physical dialogue between the two, and between the building and its larger context.

Rural settings

Villa in the wild

The Lakeside Villa, designed by Office: Kersten Geers David Van Severen in 2007, near Lake Keerbergen, Belgium, unfortunately never built, demonstrates how enclosure can be integral to the design of a single dwelling today. *Figures 2.3, 2.4, 2.5.* The formal integrity of the villa is maintained by the square geometry of the external wall, its dark polished finish reflecting back the trees of the forest on its surface. The interior spaces are all contained within a wide continuous strip of building, covered by a flat roof, leaving a smaller open square in the centre. This is entirely flooded, but at

2.3
Adaptation of basic plan.

Key

1 entrance
2 look-out tower
3 floating platform
4 sauna
5 pool garden

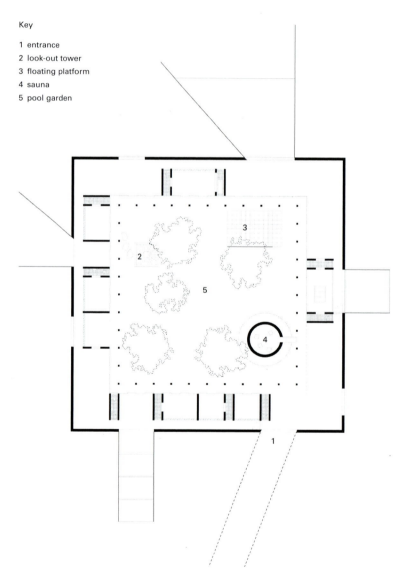

2.4
Lakeside Villa. Plan.

a depth to allow trees to grow through. The pool replaces the conventional garden, and plays on the contrast between the *wild*, the natural shape of the lake, and the *tamed*, its rationalised pure geometric form. The reflection of light filtering through the trees would light the interior, and reflect the continuous movement of the branches of the high tree canopy overhead down onto the still water and into the house. The external perimeter wall is punctured only for entry and to provide specific views that connect lake, forest and garden.

You enter through an opening that brings you underneath the roof, but open to the garden. Entry into the building itself is through a short glazed corridor that constrains your movements, giving you a view out but denying any other, until you reach a larger space where your movements are no longer restricted. This continuous free space, housing activities such as the living, dining and play area, is punctuated by a series of small separate rooms – office, bedrooms, kitchen. These, each with its own servicing area, look into the central pool/water garden.

The columns of the gridded supporting frame are exposed and provide a narrow perimeter walkway, their regular spacing contributing to the articulation of the interior façades. From one corner of the garden, stepping-stones lead you to a tower. Its staircase takes you to a lookout high in the trees. A south-facing floating terrace resides in another corner for sitting out and dining. A small pavilion, a cone-shaped sauna room, is placed in a third corner. Despite most of the garden being flooded, it can be inhabited through these small interventions.

Lakeside Villa is a re-examination of a fundamental planning principle of enclosure, poetically combining contemporary living with the essential qualities of an enclosed garden. Its strength lies in an understanding of location, in the rigour of the planning and adherence to a geometry, which, once established, allows for variations.

Within a village

The music studio, Atelier Bardill, designed by Valerio Olgiati and completed in 2007 for Linard Bardill, is an example of how enclosure has been used as a way of unifying a design at a series of different levels; through addressing the irregularities of the site, its unique location and its response to the specific brief for a music studio. It sits in the centre of the village of Scharans in Switzerland, a designated conservation area, and replaces an old barn. *Figure 2.6.* The studio takes up the equivalent overall volume of the barn, and is in scale with the other village buildings. Olgiati has researched the cultural patterns of the existing village as a reference for the new design, and reinterpretation can be seen throughout. For example, the surface treatment of the pigmented concrete wall has been crafted with hand-cut formwork, and the patterning has been worked out through collaboration between architect and builder. The reddish-brown pigmented surface gives off a warm glow, using the colour and a decorative motif traditionally used in the houses in the village. *Figure 2.7.* The design of the studio has as much to do with the given plot and understanding of site conditions as any imposed geometric rationale. As it is a very simple building that only contains the studio and the necessary services, most of the space is taken up, and monumentalised, by the garden. A large oval appears to be carved out of a flat ceiling set against the walls which have been raised up to accommodate the pitch of the roof. *Figure 2.8.* This pure geometry imposes an ordering and a power to the entire building. The studio entrance is located to the far side of the courtyard to the interior.

Coming to the studio is an event, even in this small building. First, you ascend a short flight of stairs up from street level to the front door, and then into an enclosed and powerful space, which is both warm and austere. The canopy provides protection from the elements as you negotiate your way to the doors of the studio. The wall between studio and garden is completely glazed, in contrast to the solid external boundary walls, giving you the illusion of being within the whole space and echoing the volume of the original barn. As well as enjoying the visual connection with the garden, if the sun is shining, you can observe a bright oval of light passing through the overhead opening and projecting its shape on the ground. It will slowly move across the ground plane following the sun's path as the day progresses, with complete disregard to the interior/exterior barrier made by the glass. *Figure 2.9.* Apart from the entrance, the courtyard space has only one opening, and provides a framed view of the outside world. It acts as a balcony from which you can look down into the village and across to the mountains. The slope of the ceiling and the wrapping of the double thickness wall protect and subtly change the scale. It is an indisputably twenty-first-century space, subtly referential, containing elements that are embedded within the context of the village. It has been described as

2.6
Garden surrounded by wall and building.

2.7
Atelier Bardill,
Switzerland. Looking up
the street showing the
patterned surface to the
walls.

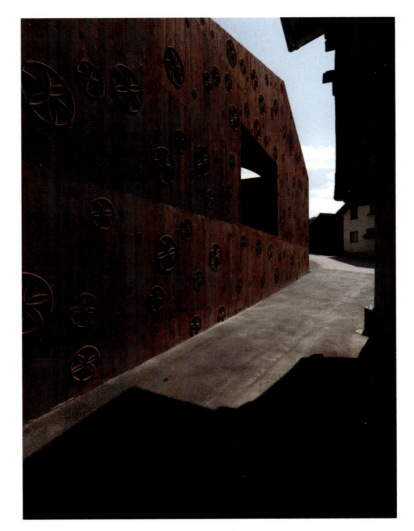

2.8
Atelier Bardill. Plan
showing the enclosed
garden with its wall taken
up to the boundary.

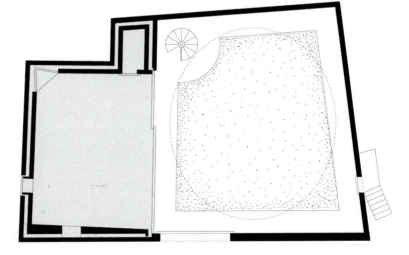

intoxicating and dream-like, but also, a place to feel comfortable in. Through
a design that Olgiati describes as an 'indivisible totality',[1] it has the grandeur
of a palace, combined with simplicity and introspectiveness.

The urban environment

Housing in the nineteenth and twentieth centuries, through expediency, has
favoured terraced housing,[2] with deep plans and back gardens on long plots.
Enclosed gardens have been out of favour, and been substituted by the
back garden. With inventiveness, even quite narrow plots can be exploited
to insert enclosed gardens that transform the quality of space.

Terrace

Eduardo Souto de Moura designed a group of nine terraced houses at
Matosinhos, Portugal, in 1993, where the houses have long thin plots, and
open spaces within them have been designed into the scheme from the
start. *Figure 2.10*. They fit into the old vegetable garden of a villa, which has
been surrounded by the now expanding town. The design has evolved from
a detailed reading of the context of the area, including individual dwellings.

Despite the change of use from garden to housing, Souto de Moura
has maintained the presence of elements of the site that make it unique.
It is a very tranquil scheme. The design was driven by his desire to utilise
the wall, 'to build walls, a characteristic feature of the area. The Portuguese
house is the continuation of the wall around it, and sometimes the only

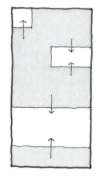

2.10
Three open spaces within
the boundary.

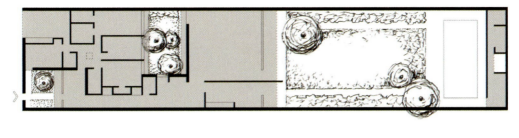

2.11
Matosinhos, Portugal. Plan of one of the terraced houses, indicating the series of courtyard spaces, from public to private, carved into a regular rectilinear terrace.

2.12
Matosinhos. Courtyard housing, making use of vernacular and contemporary use of material. The discreet entrance gives nothing away.

sign from the road of the presence of the house is a window'.[3] The plots are divided with parallel walls, and a wall wraps around the entire plot of nine. They are over-sailed by strips of concrete that make up the roof over all the houses running at right angles to the long plots. An apparent gap between wall and roof prevents any interruption to the integrity of the wall.

The enclosing walls are absolute. As soon as you enter the first patio of any of the houses, square in plan, you are immediately cut off and enter a separate world, very quiet and still, stripped down, in stark contrast to the adjacent busy main road and harbour. *Figure 2.11*. You enter the building and the layout of the rooms suggests a journey articulated by varying qualities of light. You are drawn through to the living area which looks onto another patio, this time stretching the entire width of the plot. Several of the houses have swimming pools, and the garden is enclosed at the rear with buildings associated with the pool and garden maintenance. The wall facing the patio is fully glazed, giving maximum visual contact with the garden, whilst a deep canopy prevents direct sunlight coming inside and overheating the living areas. The large patio doors give direct access to the garden. The more private areas of the house are separated discreetly by a door towards the middle of the house, and the bedrooms all look onto a third patio, hidden and very secluded.

The house embodies architectural modernism in its lack of decoration or ornament, its strict geometric articulation of spaces and planar connections between roof, wall and floor. It has a restricted pallet of materials. Load-bearing walls with a rendered finish are used internally and granite, reflecting the walls of the old garden, is used on the public façades. The scheme refers to the historical precedent of the Moorish occupation of the Middle Ages, turning its back on the street and entering the private world of the dwelling, brought to life through the subtle modulation of light. *Figure 2.12.*

Adaptation and transformation

In the inter-war period in Britain, the semi-detached version of the terrace was much in demand. Despite there being more space around a dwelling, it was not well utilised. Re-examination of this type has led to inventive solutions to the problems, particularly light and access, caused by the long, thin plot.

The White House was built in the 1920s and converted by Pierre d'Avoine in 1992. It demonstrates how an enclosed garden can be made even in a tightly packed row of houses, and how the quality of interior spaces, originally dark, can be enhanced and transformed through adaption of the existing layout. It also demonstrates how small external spaces can come to life through economy of means and the making of an enclosed external space.

The house appears to be like any of the other 1920s semi-detached houses in a quiet suburban London street but, as you enter, the light quality immediately feels different and you have a sense of having entered the late twentieth century. *Figure 2.13.* D'Avoine, through much discussion with his clients and severe space restriction, has given new life to the house by opening up the interior. By extending out across most of the width of the plot at the back, he has created a small courtyard garden out of a neglected back yard at the side. *Figure 2.14.* Wherever you turn there are views of either the garden or the new courtyard, placed adjacent to the dining area. On warm days, or even when there is a glimmer of sun on cooler days, the sliding doors can be pushed open and you can walk through to a

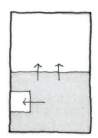

2.13
Two open spaces within the boundary.

2.14
The White House, London.
Ground floor plans. Before
and after showing leftover
spaces at the side have
been shaped, and become
an extension of the living
area.

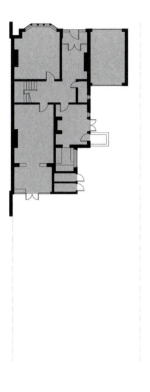
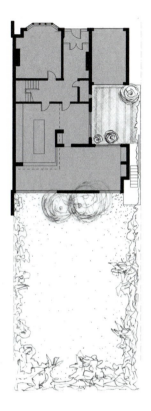

compact but comfortably proportioned outdoor room. Best use has been
made of the orientation of the house, which is at the end of the terrace,
facing north at the rear. The west-facing little courtyard is glazed on two
sides, giving the interior access to direct sunlight in the afternoon and early
evening. By placing an opening in the south-facing wall to the extended
living area, sunlight can fall directly through into what would otherwise be
an entirely north-lit room. It also provides a visual connection between
courtyard and garden. *Figures 2.15, 2.16.*

A further connection is made at first-floor level. Two of the rooms
now lead directly onto a steel balcony which takes you to a pivoted stair
that leads directly down to the rear garden above the access path. The upper
walkway and its encompassing steel-framed structure provide cohesion to
the mixture of old and new aspects of the house, and gives the illusion of
a canopy overhead when you are at ground floor level, without cutting down
the light from above. The two very enclosed outdoor areas are complementary opposites. The courtyard is light and full of potted plants and
creepers, and has been paved to make a detailed warm pattern of concrete,

From patio to park

stone and oak. The white painted walls give it an inviting freshness. A simple screen has been placed along the boundary beside the extension, which is now covered in ivy, growing so vigorously that it is in danger of consuming it. As well as providing privacy it makes a connection between this space and the very sheltered enclosed rear garden, which is entirely created by foliage, and makes a transition from a small ordered patch of paradise through to a sultry, verdant arcadia.

Refuge

The Maggie's Centre at Charing Cross Hospital, London, designed by Rogers Stirk Harbour and Partners, opened in 2008. The design of the building demonstrates how enclosure and the inclusion of several enclosed gardens has played a significant part in developing the character of building which is domestic in scale, despite its connection with a large hospital. The garden spaces are important in creating the atmosphere of a healing environment, and the building provides a safe haven for patients within the hospital grounds. *Figure 2.17.*

2.17
Three open spaces within the boundary.

The Centre, sits on the corner of a large site in the middle of London. Despite its difficult location, sandwiched between busy roads and the vast hospital building complex, it is a haven of calm. The Maggie's Centre initiative, championed by Charles Jencks, was set up after his wife Maggie Keswick died of cancer in 1993. This and a growing number of other Maggie's Centres have been built to provide a place of refuge for cancer patients. They are designed specifically to be non-institutional, and different from the high-tech sterile environment of the hospitals they are attached to, where efficiency and hygiene have been drivers of often very dehumanised environments.

Emphasis has been put on the 'feel' of the place as well as its functionality. It is a modestly scaled building, but being coloured bright red it is unmissable, and stands out against the monotones of the hospital buildings and the urban grain of the street. *Figure 2.18.* As you approach it through a tranquil and domestic-scale garden, a projecting wall draws you in, past a plain façade with a single opening in it. As you get closer, you see that the space behind it is a garden. You are welcomed into a series of interlinked domestically scaled spaces. Nothing is overbearing. Most noticeably, the gardens have been brought inside. The largest one sits entirely within the envelope of the building directly adjacent to the dining and kitchen area. *Figure 2.19.* You are aware of it from much of the ground floor and can even look down on it from the roof terrace garden on the first floor. The centrally placed table and benches seem to send an invitation to go out and sit on them. *Figure 2.20.*

In all, there are four small gardens, tightly packed within the confines of a rectilinear envelope. The inclusion of the gardens, together with warm

2.18
Approach to the Maggie's Centre, showing the enclosing wall and oversailing roof.

2.19
Ground floor plan of the Maggie's Centre, London, showing the integration of external and internal spaces within the envelope of the building. The building has a protecting line of birch trees on the street side, and the domestic-scale garden on the entrance side. The garden reappears internally as integral to the functioning of the building.

colours and timber finishes of the interior and the informality of the interior spaces themselves create a unique atmosphere.

The building has an over-sailing roof that appears to hover over the greater part of it, with triangular cut-outs in place, bringing light directly down to the interior. Its separation from the external walls provides adequate light for plants to grow healthily in the smaller spaces as well as letting light in at first-floor level. It acts as a canopy and gives unity to this small building.

As Jenks and Heathcote[4] discuss in their book celebrating Maggie's Centres, the design is undeniably modernist in its approach. It has also overcome some of the pitfalls of modernism where visual considerations have dominated designs. Despite the rectilinear shape of the overall plan, the inclusion of garden areas has provided a dialogue with nature throughout, even within relatively small spaces, and has taken the building beyond the simple box.

2.20
Maggie's Centre. Looking through to the main courtyard.

Medium

A still centre

The placing of a garden within a medium-sized building complex with multiple rooms has proved to be a useful strategy. The garden provides a fixed point around which the building can be designed, providing access and a natural light source in a deep plan. If the weather is warm enough it can be used as another habitable space. It also contributes to its character, a still centre that brings us in close contact with the natural world and the changing seasons.

Clare Hall, designed by Ralph Erskine, completed in 1969, is a graduate college at the University of Cambridge. *Figure 2.21.* The architect has acknowledged and respected the evolution of the development of university buildings in Cambridge, but has designed the college to be appropriate to the needs of staff and students of the twentieth century. Students with families are accommodated, and parking has been provided for a limited number of cars underneath the building. The main block is a deep plan (*Figure 2.22*) comprising a split-level open area for students, and smaller cellular rooms for staff. Shortly after you have entered the building, and turn to your right, you encounter a completely internalised garden.

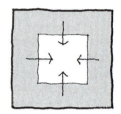

2.21
Single central open space.

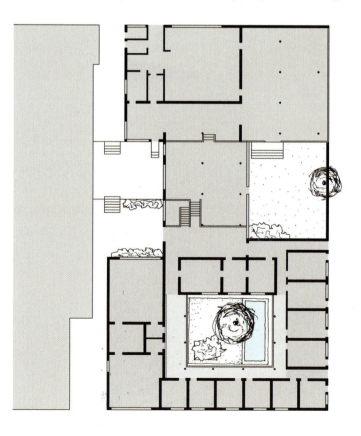

2.22
Clare Hall, Cambridge, UK.
Ground floor plan.

Figure 2.23. Although it is now over 40 years old, the encircling corridor is very modern and light. The garden wall is glazed on three sides, and slender pale laminated timber columns hold up the roof, tapering at the top and bottom. It also has the air of being constantly inhabited. People gather and talk, and it is a regular venue for exhibitions. *Figure 2.24.* When the weather permits the doors are opened, providing access to the garden for staff and students. There is a small fountain that can just be heard from

2.23
Internal garden in the heart of Clare Hall.

2.24
Clare Hall. Corridor surrounding the garden.

inside, enticing you to seek it out. A rain collector is made into a sculptural feature that naturally replenishes the pond. The garden combines an active space (interior), with one of calm (garden), which is central to the atmosphere of the college. As staff and students carry out their daily activities, this small encounter with nature helps provide an awareness of not just the changing quality of light throughout the seasons but also of the atmosphere that only planting can provide.

As an additive process

A closed system

The device used at Clare Hall can be traced back to the cloister garden of a monastery. The layout of the simple enclosed garden – once established as a strategy for designing – can be repeated, generating large building complexes. The Carthusian monastery at Pavia in Italy shows such an ever-expanding plan. It is situated on a relatively flat site in open countryside where unimpeded expansion could take place. The planning developed orthogonally, providing orderly regulated spaces that reflect the aspirations of monastic life. Using the same principles of expansion and enclosure, a range of similar types of enclosed gardens have been made. There is a grand cloister garden to the south of the main church, and then a series of other cloister gardens proliferate beyond it, surrounded by rooms that are required to support the whole community. *Figure 2.25*. The monastery was

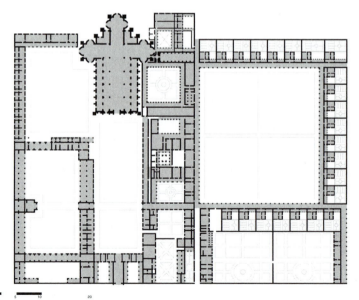

2.25
Plan of the Certosa at Pavia, showing the uninterrupted rectilinear planning based on series of cloistered gardens that range from the very formal public cloister behind the church to the gardens of the individual monks' dwellings. Circulation is through the use of covered cloister walkways.

From patio to park

2.26

Sketch of monks' houses and enclosed gardens that together wrap around the largest cloister garden. Within the Carthusian Order each monk had his own quarters to live in, with an external loggia that looked onto his own individual enclosed garden for him to tend and as a place for private contemplation.

entirely self-sufficient, and all aspects of living needed to be catered for – cooking and eating, prayer, work, tending the sick. Each garden was the centre of the activities around it. They ranged from the scale of the private individual dwelling where each monk had his own dwelling and garden, designed for what today we would call minimal living, to the more functional spaces such as the herbarium, where plants were grown for cooking and remedies, or the communal ceremonial space of the main cloister.

The monastery, with its covered walkways, is the result of a straightforward design principle that relies on both building and garden. The rectilinear circulation connects spaces and rooms through a repeating pattern, part of a continuous method of space and place-making that together provide continuity and a sense of unity of the whole. *Figure 2.26*.

An evolving system

As education spread in Western Europe during the Middle Ages, the monastic plan was deemed suitable for educational institutions. It was easily adapted to have a greater emphasis on study rather than prayer, but still maintained an austerity matching the seriousness of academic life. There are many examples of the continuous use of this pattern, up to and including the present day, despite changing attitudes toward education, building design, and changing pace of student life.

To walk into the courts of St John's College, Cambridge, UK is like architectural time travelling, passing through a series of stage sets. You pass through a wicket gate set in the main doors away from the bustling street into the oldest part of the college, First Court, which was started in the sixteenth century. *Figure 2.27*. You are in a grand open room, with a carpeting of immaculately maintained lawns. The atmosphere is calm. The noise from the street has diminished, and the space, bounded by the exterior walls of the buildings, has no distractions, no fountains, bushes or herbaceous borders. You continue through a patchwork of successive

2.27
St John's College,
Cambridge. First Court,
planted only with lawns.

courts,[5] which have been added as the college has expanded. The architecture changes, expressing each century's ideas and preoccupations, but the basic layout has been maintained, providing consistency through the planning and type of the spaces. A pattern of movement develops, of being squeezed into a confined space as you pass through the buildings, such as the space between the Great Hall and the kitchens, and then of release as you move into the next court and along cloistered walkways.

By the time you reach New Court you have arrived at the twentieth century. *Figure 2.28*. You look onto the façade of the Cripps Building, designed by architects Powell and Moya, 1963–67. Although the space is

2.28
Cripps Building, St John's
College. Walkway and
access at ground level.

2.29
Aerial view of St John's
College, indicating the
progression from the
street from First Court
through to New Court and
the Cripps Building.

2.30
Cripps Building walkway,
access to stairways to
students' bedrooms.

open at one end, the building wraps around the space, joining up with the Fischer Building, completing the enclosure. By adhering to the established planning principles, the design has maintained a coherence and spatial continuity already established throughout the complex. *Figure 2.29.* Student rooms look onto the central court, and access to them is along a covered passage, a modernist interpretation of the cloister, faced with Portland stone, and with reinforced concrete and steel stairs as access to the rooms. *Figure 2.30.*

Vertical planning

Enclosed gardens do not necessarily need to be at ground level. An increasing number of gardens are appearing on the flat roofs of buildings, particularly where land at ground level is scarce. In temperate climates green roofs are considered not only to be good for the environment, but can also be used by the occupants of the building.

An elevated 'meadow' has been included in the design of the School of Music at the Polytechnic Institute in Lisbon, designed by João Luís Carrilho da Graça, 1998–2008. The architects' main reference is the cloister at Pavia, surrounded by the monks' individual dwellings. *Figures 2.31, 2.32.* The building makes an uncompromising bold statement in an area of suburban Lisbon, adjacent to a major arterial road where planning and integrity of urban space is hard to find. On a limited site it has exploited the idea of enclosure both vertically as well as horizontally. The building, on three floors, is strictly rectilinear in plan and sits on a sloping site. The mid level is centred around a large and stark courtyard that connects both to the outside entrance area, and the top floor via an external stair. *Figure 2.33.* The steps lead you directly onto the 'meadow', which fills the centre of the upper level of the building. It is richly planted, but kept at a low level, and can be read as a plane of greenery, a deep-pile carpet, patterned with flowers, offset by the neutral background of the white rendered building and considerably more exuberant than the controlled lawns of Cambridge. *Figure 2.34.*

The individual music practice rooms all look onto this central space. The scale is comparable to that of the monks' cloister in Pavia. It sits on top of the main concert hall. Circulation has been placed around the perimeter walls, reversing the monastic model in this case. The original plan was for the building to be surrounded by a ring of planting, nature wrapping around the building, a transitional zone between building and suburb, buffering the sounds from the busy roads and streets, as we have seen at the Maggie's Centre, but unfortunately that has not been executed to date.

2.31
Circulation around the outside perimeter.

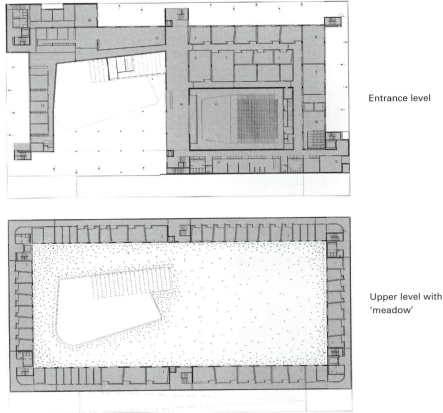

Entrance level

Upper level with internal 'meadow'

2.32
School of Music, Polytechnic Institute, Lisbon. Plans of central and upper level. Individual practice rooms all look onto the enclosed garden.

2.33
School of Music, Lisbon.
Central level.

2.34
School of Music, Lisbon.
The 'meadow'.

Threshold

Enclosed gardens mediate between public and private areas within a city by creating an intermediate zone between the street, and the interior of a building.

This is clearly demonstrated at the Louis-Jeantet Research Institute in Geneva, designed by Agence TER. A sunken enclosed garden is used as a foyer space for a new lecture theatre.[6] *Figures 2.35, 2.36.* It lies

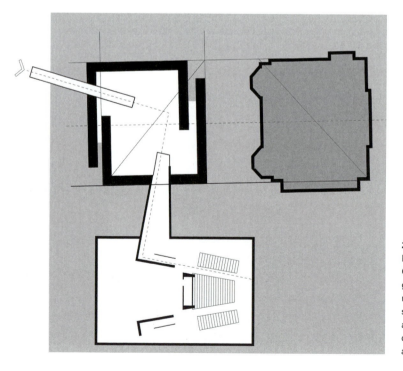

2.35
Louis-Jeantet Institute, Geneva. Plan of lower garden court showing the ramp descending from the street and angled to accommodate a change in direction into the auditorium.

2.36
Louis-Jeantet Institute, Geneva. Section showing sunken garden in relation to the street, existing house and entrance to the new auditorium.

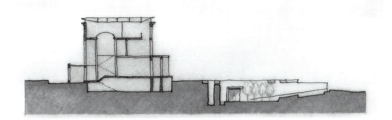

between the busy street and the hidden interior world of an auditorium. The garden of the adjacent building has been dug out, but retains a plinth at the upper garden level. A ramp invites you down from the street into the lowered garden through a hole in the boundary wall. As you descend and the city noises recede, you hear water splashing down steps from channels let into the surrounding walls. You are directed to the main entrance, a cave-like opening along the adjacent wall. In their book *The Enclosed Garden*, Aben and de Wit[7] discuss how 'the garden does duty as a decompression chamber, filtering the sounds of the city, and its welter of imagery'. *Figure 2.37*. The ramp slows you down, and the space itself,

2.37
Louis-Jeantet Institute, Geneva. View of sunken garden.

with its sparse planting, acts as a filter and prepares you for a further reduction of sensual deprivation within the auditorium. The subtlety of this scheme lies largely in the juxtaposition of two grids.[8] One is derived from the boundary wall of the garden that respects the existing boundaries of the houses along the street and the morphology of the city. The other intersecting grid is a reflection of how people use and travel through the space and provides a path to the auditorium entrance.

You might well miss the entrance to the National Museum of Contemporary Art in the historic Chiado area of Lisbon, renovated in 1994 by Jean Michel Wilmotte. There is a high wall running against the side of a narrow pavement with a modest entrance door within it. You enter and rise up a flight of steps to find yourself within a courtyard surrounded by contemporary buildings. They are new wings added to the original Convent of Sao Francisco. *Figure 2.38.*

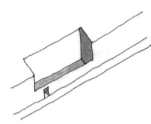

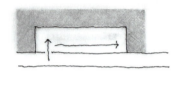

2.38
Museum of Contemporary Art, Chiado, Lisbon. Diagram showing relationship with street. Access is up to an elevated garden.

2.39
Museum of Contemporary Art, Chiado, Lisbon. Looking toward the entrance. A rill leading from a small pool set in the paving leads to the main entrance.

From patio to park

The courtyard garden, well above street level, provides some breathing space for visitors to orient themselves after the noisy and somewhat chasm-like streets of the city. It acts as a place to pause, in preparation for either visiting the art gallery or returning back to the city. A café invites you to linger a little longer. The modern patio garden of lawn and paving is a very sympathetic setting for the display of art works. There are no bushes or trees to distract from the art. *Figures 2.39, 2.40.* A rill cut into the paving indicates direction and runs along a processional route to the main entrance, and the thick boundary wall cuts out the noise and pollution from the city. It is regularly pierced with large cone-shaped openings that you can look down back at the street and across to the rest of the city.

2.40
Museum of Contemporary Art, Chiado, Lisbon. A reminder of the city. A series of portholes give glimpses of the city, as if through the lens of a camera.

Large

Urban greenery – breathing spaces in the city

Public gardens in the city are enjoyed for their contrast to the urban environment and contribute to the quality of our urban lives. We often talk of them as the city's 'green lungs'. Blocks of buildings provide the boundaries of these breathing spaces. They are often called city rooms, whether they are squares or gardens. The survival of city gardens, some of which date back several centuries, such as Lincoln's Inn Fields in London, is testimony to the importance of the need and desire for contact with nature in the city. Enclosed public city gardens give a range of opportunities for bringing calm out of chaos. Their spatial coherence favours stasis rather than movement, and can slow down our pace. They can also be landmarks, seen from a distance in contrast to their built-up surroundings. They can be events in their own right, or markers on a journey, spaces to expand into. They can be gathering places or somewhere for us to pause before continuing to our next destination.

Planned city gardens

Enclosure within the city block

The interior spaces of city blocks are often inaccessible. In many European cities pedestrians are occasionally given a view through an archway into a private courtyard, often full of plants, with a very different quality of light to the street. They look very enticing, and even if we cannot gain access, these spaces add to our imaginative appreciation of the city.

However, public access is not always denied. At the end of the eighteenth century the Palais Royal in Paris was converted from a ducal palace to a public garden. It is situated within an entire urban block and is not revealed from the street. It is a very formally planned rectilinear garden, large enough to contain avenues of trees, and a large central park full of formal gardens and fountains. Despite much scepticism it was an instant success. *Figure 2.41.* A great variety of entertainments flourished both in the garden and in the buildings. At ground-floor level there was a variety of commercial enterprises, and rooms for the more risqué activities, gambling houses and brothels, were more discreetly located upstairs. It included a theatre at each end. From the start, people from all walks of life have walked through it for the pleasure of the garden itself. It was in constant demand: money was made, and people were entertained as they still are today. It is a place to be inhabited as part of the urban experience,

2.41
Palais Royal, Paris. Aerial view indicating its scale within the city, and its complete enclosure within a city block, its entrances at both ends connecting north and south and the lining of avenues of trees along its west and east side.

2.42
The gardens of the Palais Royal have a long history as a meeting place in the heart of Paris: a rendezvous for shoppers, concert goers, performances in the gardens, for drinking and assignations on the upper floors. Even on a chilly November morning when this photograph was taken it was full of people.

with much of its success relying on the concentration of activities that the space itself inspires.

It is very grand, and owes much of its success to its spatial coherence and layered boundaries. Nowadays it is also an important pedestrian link within the heart of the city. The outer boundary consists of arcaded galleries at ground level, containing shops, restaurants and a theatre, but now with offices and residential units above. The configuration of open arcades makes the façade a spatially interactive plane rather than an impenetrable solid wall. The consistency of the architecture, its regularity and proportion in relation to the open space, gives it orderliness and cohesion. Rows of trees provide it with an inner lining. The longer north/south sides are each flanked by two avenues of lime trees that provide shady paths to promenade along, away from the bustling street. Although they are lower in height than the architecture, they make a bold formal statement, clipped with precision. They become a continuous overhead canopy, the columns of orderly tree trunks below mediating between building and nature. The central space is divided into a series of different gardens, shaped by shrubs and fountains. The scale is small enough for us to be conscious of the formal components surrounding them, and enjoy the intimacy of the smaller scale. The entire garden invites you to participate and join in the action, and despite the grandeur of the whole, you are never intimidated. *Figure 2.42.*

Enclosure within the city

Enclosed gardens were designed in the original planning of much of the new residential areas of eighteenth-century London. Bloomsbury, for example, is characterised by its regular blocks of terraced houses that fit into an orderly pattern of streets, squares and gardens. Their growth and popularity arose from an increasing pressure for residential development from prosperous land-owners who wished to come to London from the country for 'the season', a period every year when society parties and dinners took place.[9] Property developers divided up lots that included open squares acting as centrepieces, magnets[10] for the wealthy purchaser, after which the lesser streets were constructed. Some squares contained gardens, enclosed with railings, and accessible only to residents. As all the houses looked onto the garden there was a sense of joint ownership. The inhabitants of the square had the advantage of being seen publicly as soon as they walked out of their front door, with an elegant architectural statement of their residence behind them. They also enjoyed the exclusive use of the garden that took up the greater part of the square, a reminder of the countryside they had left behind. Gardens and architecture contributed to the theatre of the city. *Figures 2.43, 2.44.*

The uniformity of the terraces, with their flat façades and straight horizontal parapets read as single planes, make clearly defined boundaries to the spaces. Despite the gardens' substantial size, with some very mature trees within them now, the background of the terraces is always present. Neither garden nor building dominates. The natural forms of the planting offset the regular pattern and proportions of the architecture. All the main rooms of the houses, raised several steps up from ground level, look out to a view of a contrived natural landscape. In Bedford Square, because the garden is designed as an oval placed within a rectangle, there is plenty of room between the façades of the buildings and the garden itself to observe

2.43
Sketch plan of Bedford Square, London.

the garden as a whole. The success of these spaces can also be measured by the current real estate value of the houses, and very few people can now afford to use them as homes. The houses have proved to be adaptable for a range of uses, and are mainly occupied by successful commercial businesses. Although there is a sense of privilege and ownership for the people working there, the gardens make a large contribution to the openness and accessibility of the city and many of the squares are open now to the public.

Evolved spaces in the city

As part of the city

Areas that have evolved over time through the changing pattern of city life often have as strong a character as those that have been planned. In many cases it is the interweaving of the spaces between the buildings that provides coherence.

The Inns of Court, traditionally the legal centre of London, and much celebrated in many of Charles Dickens's novels, are no exception. They stretch from the Thames Embankment northward to Gray's Inn in an unbroken pedestrian promenade of gardens and courtyards in one of the densest parts of the city. Instead of the rigid pattern of a single institution, or the formal planning of Bloomsbury, spaces connect discreetly with building and garden appearing to mould around each other. Although the area has had many face-lifts much of the layout has been unaffected by time. Despite the variety of configuration of architectural style and proportion, the area

2.45
Inns of Court. The gardens
are used as much by
people working in the
offices as by people
travelling through.

as a whole maintains its own particular atmosphere, characterised by the gardens. Each garden, different from, but linked to its neighbour, is immaculately maintained, and responds to the architecture immediately surrounding it. Building materials such as stone, brick and slate and timber have weathered well.

Although the spaces are privately owned, pedestrians have free access. *Figure 2.47.* These beautiful gardens cannot fail to be appreciated by anyone who is walking through. They provide a less frenetic world to the street, where you can have a conversation without having to raise your voice, and even hear a bird sing. The journey, like the university route, creates a pattern of open and constrained movement as you travel through a garden, through a passage in a building, under an archway, across a courtyard, or squeeze past two adjacent buildings.

The authenticity of the Inns of Court, so steeped in the past, might well be questioned. There is no doubt that there is a preciousness to it, but its consistent and continuing use as a working environment has helped keep it alive. When you pass through you do not feel so much like a tourist looking into a museum, but more a *flaneur,*[11] let into a scene of the interior life of the city. *Figure 2.45.*

Sanctuary

A city by definition is a busy place, full of action night and day. For many of us, respite is as necessary as engagement. One of the secrets of many old towns is the hidden spaces contained within them.

You feel privileged to enter the garden of the Begijnhof, located in the centre of Amsterdam. Seven centuries ago it was inhabited by a sisterhood

2.46
Inward looking central
space.

2.47
Inns of Court, London. Plan showing a continuous passage of accessible gardens in the heart of the city.

who worked in the community without taking any monastic vows. They returned to this sanctuary after their labours for the sick and needy were finished at the end of each day. It has been inhabited ever since. Discrete narrow passages lead off from the main thoroughfares into the sanctuary. *Figure 2.48.* You walk into a surprisingly large, irregularly shaped open space, containing a well-tended garden and a small church, completely enclosed by tall and narrow houses, typical of the seventeenth and eighteenth centuries. After treading on the muted greys of the city floor, you move into an outdoor room covered with a soft green carpet of lawns. It feels very private and there is an implication of ownership by the inhabitants of the encircling houses that face into it. *Figures 2.49, 2.50.* Although their heights vary from between three and five storeys, and each is different to the next and individually designed, there is overall consistency. This is achieved mainly through the

2.48
Begijnhof, Amsterdam. Entrance. The door is locked at night.

From patio to park

2.50
Begijnhof, Amsterdam.
The garden is completely
hidden from the streets.

use of a limited palette of colour and materials, the uniform fenestration, the rhythm of the gable ends, the alignment of façades and the irregular convex curve of the whole space through the positioning of each block.

The case studies provide a small window into the wealth of designs that are derived from the basic principle of enclosure, where garden and architecture complement each other, one providing the context for the other, whether it is at the scale of an individual dwelling, an institution or the city.

From patio to park

3 Taming nature –

and the way to Paradise

Oasis

We had travelled for several hours on dirt roads laid over expanses of sand and rock, on our way to a small oasis village, Toconao, in the middle of the Atacama Desert in northern Chile. It is one of the driest places on earth, a high and virtually rainless plateau, stretching 600 miles from north to south, and spanning between the Andes and the Pacific coast. There had been virtually no vegetation visible during the entire journey from San Pedro, the town where we were based. The only signs of life were flocks of brilliant pink flamingos that have been able to adapt themselves to take sustenance from the crustaceans that live in an expansive salt lake, one of the major geographical features of this strange landscape that reminded us of images of the moon, rather than of South America.

There was nothing exceptional about the village, with its white-washed church and adobe houses, but before we left, we were encouraged to walk down a path that appeared to take us straight back into a cleft in the desert. We started to notice more undergrowth, and then came across larger bushes lining the path that provided some shade, which was a great relief from the heat of the sun and dryness of the atmosphere. We were walking into a deep and narrow valley, carved out by a stream flowing from the high Andes down to a plateau that lay behind the village. *Figure 3.1.* The valley's steep sides sheltered its floor despite the high angle of the sun, and by now there was a rich variety of luxuriant trees and shrubs. It was a shock to us after the desert. We walked along the stream for about twenty minutes and then sat down on its banks where they broadened out.

There we were, sitting in dappled light under the trees, with quince blossom above us, the sound of running water from the stream, birds singing, and the breeze passing through the branches overhead making a slight rustle, and cooling us from the searing heat of the day; and yet we were in the middle of a vast desert. Scarlet pomegranates lay scattered in the under-growth. We felt we had stumbled into Paradise. *Figure 3.2.* I later learnt that the technical term for it is a quebrada, a geographical feature of the desert that produces oasis conditions. After a picnic lunch we wandered further into the valley and discovered that most of it was cultivated and had an internal organisational structure of its own. Areas were fenced off into gardens and orchards and a variety of crops were being grown. We stepped over a complex system of sluiced irrigation channels surrounding the plots, and the gentle music of the stream or the gushing of the channelled water pouring down the terraces was always present. *Figures 3.3, 3.4.* As we peered through the latticework gates of each plot we could see that many of them had tables and chairs, ready for processing and preparing and eating food. The pathway led us to an opening beside the stream containing benches and a large stone hearth that had the air of long-established regular use.

We stayed for a while, reflecting on the delicious sensuous experience and taste of Paradise, before returning to the heat and dust of the village. Far from it being an excursion for tourists, the quebrada was an orderly area of used land, marked out and made fertile through the use of a regulated irrigation system and making a series of individual enclosed gardens; allotments where fruits, flowers and vegetables can be grown. It was also

3.2
The steep sides of the
quebrada shelter the
interior, making a natural
enclosed garden. The floor
of the valley is fertile
enough for plants to be
cultivated.

3.3
Quebrada. Sluices redirect
water to ensure that all
plots are equally irrigated.

3.4
Quebrada. Gate into one
of the allotments on the
valley floor. Vegetation is
used to make a part-living
threshold.

3.5
Diagrammatic section
through a quebrada.

an important part of the community, a place to come to and, through
nurturing the vegetation, enjoy a contrasting environment to the village. It
was a natural enclosed garden for people to meet and feast in. The quebrada
is an enclosed garden that has been designed by nature. *Figure 3.5.*

A developing idea

This chapter will look at the development of enclosed gardens from early
enclosures to their growing metaphorical significance – particularly through
their association with Paradise – by tracing their lineage through Persian,
Roman and Islamic origins.

Eden and Paradise

The fertile oasis is one of the most important constituents of life in the desert, a place to escape the relentless heat. It is the one place that provides shape and form within an endless formless landscape.[1] It is a reminder of a much wider phenomenon – of secure areas where plants grow that provide sustenance, and can be enjoyed in the midst of wilder inhospitable zones. As such places are essential for survival, it is not surprising that we attribute great significance to them and that we have constructed our own equivalent oases elsewhere.

The sacred notion of Paradise, a place where we can transcend our human frailty, has been central to many cultures for many centuries. In Judaism, Christianity and Islam the very first garden was the Garden of Eden, a place, somewhere on earth, where our ancestors were in direct contact with God, before they were forced out into the wilderness. There was a desire to get back to this place of perfection, where we want for nothing, where there is plenty, where it is perpetual springtime, and life is eternal. There was also a widely held belief that having been thrown out of the Garden of Eden, we may seek redemption and aim to find an alternative solution. 'God, while ejecting Adam from the Garden of Eden, had, in his mercy, been preparing for an even better home, or Paradise'.[2] It was also believed in medieval Europe that the Garden of Eden existed as a tangible place on earth, and that it would eventually be found. Its location was indicated on maps such as the Mappa Mundi in Hereford Cathedral, UK, in a location toward the East. The fifteenth-century Fra Mauro map of the world has a perspectival representation of the Garden of Eden inset within the whole picture, but outside the central circular section which is devoted to a two-dimensional map of the world. *Figure 3.6*. Eden is shown to be within a high enclosing wall. A stream flows out from within, to a less idealised place; a depiction of the known world. The stream divides into four; the four rivers that divide up the four continents. The Garden of Eden in both maps is shown as contained within the pure geometry of a cylindrical wall.

Paradise evolving

'I want to tell you about a garden, the great hunting park of an Assyrian king', Jean whispered later, in the darkness of Lucjan's kitchen. 'Fragrant groves of cedar and box, oak and fruit trees, bowers of jasmine and illuru, iris and anemone, camomile and daisy, crocus, poppy and the lily both wild and cultivated, on the banks of the Tigris. Blossoms swaying in a hot sunlight of scent, great hazy banks of shimmering perfume, a moving wall of scent.'

Anne Michaels, *The Winter Vault*[3]

3.6
Detail of the fifteenth-
century Fra Mauro map
of the world showing the
Garden of Eden placed
outside the known world.

The word paradise is the transliteration of the Old Persian word, *Pairidaeza*,[4] literally meaning a place surrounded by walls, that was used long before the biblical accounts. It appears in some of the first texts ever to be written down, in the Sumerian period in Mesopotamia. A Pairidaeza was either an enclosed hunting ground, or a designated area where land in the middle of the desert was made fertile enough to support human habitation, through the distribution of water from the Tigris and the Euphrates and their tributaries. This created many possibilities. If shade and shelter can be provided, and if water can be utilised effectively and efficiently, if invaders can be kept out, we are left with a secure area for animals to graze, or for crops to grow.

The earliest recorded Persian garden dates back to 546 BCE; a geometrically designed plot which complemented and united the official and residential buildings of Cyrus the Great. The Greek essayist and historian Xenophon, in his Socratic discourse *Oeconomicus*[5] tells us that the Persian king is not only brilliant at the art of war, but also at the art of cultivation. There is archaeological evidence of an orderly park, an enclosure that contained rows of trees which enclose an irrigated garden.[6] By the third century BCE the Babylonians describe Divine Paradise as a garden. Cultivation had risen to the status of art, expressing the values of that society. Just as architecture is a means of expression beyond the necessities of shelter, so gardens started to be seen as a means for expressing ideas of the sacred and of human aspiration toward perfection – to be appreciated by owners and occupiers – for needs other than those met by the production of food. This understanding of the garden as more than a place of utility is the point of departure for a wealth of designs where architecture and garden enclosure enjoy an intimate relationship, and one that has withstood and transcended considerable cultural and geographical difference.

Roman foundations

The peristyle garden

There is much archaeological evidence that suggests a desire to be close to nature in our everyday lives. The enclosed garden was an integral part of the Roman domestic house. The *peristyle* house, with its interior garden, was a very popular and versatile dwelling type. The building envelope of town houses was usually taken up to the plot boundary, and this meant that access to daylight could only be from above. Two types of top-lit spaces evolved: the atrium at the front of the house, and the peristyle garden at the rear.

The axial location of these spaces made it possible to see right through from the street, creating spatial continuity right to the back of the plot. *Figure 3.7.* People could walk past one of these homes and not only see the garden, but see a framed view of the family. This organisation of rooms and open spaces within the house made a theatre of the lives of others, a perfect setting for displaying wealth and even a fashion statement. *Figures 3.8, 3.9.* The view was seen through a series of spaces: the vestibule, atrium and tablinum and finally the garden. The garden itself would

3.7
Pompeii. Looking directly through from the entrance vestibule, across the atrium to the peristyle garden.

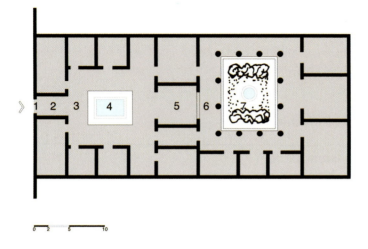

3.8
Roman town house.
Typical layout.

Key: Typical Roman Villa

1 Street entrance
2 Vestibule
3 Atrium
4 Impluvium
5 Tabernum
6 Peristyle
7 Garden

have been lined with a colonnade, the *peristyle*. It was planted with shrubs and trees, either in the ground, or in pots. Vitruvius in his treatise on architecture commented on the virtues of greenery.[7] He also discussed gardens as having a certain status: 'The open-air spaces between the colonnades should be embellished with greenery because walks out of doors are very healthy, for the air from greenery is rarefied.'[8] *Figure 3.10*.

Colonnades gave the Romans protection from the excesses of the weather and provided an area where women could carry out certain types of work that were deemed suitable to their status. The garden could be stocked with plants for display, food, or medicinal herbs, and the pond might contain fish for the dinner table.[9] It was also the perfect venue for a party.

3.9
Visual link between spaces.

3.10
House in Pompeii, now used as a café, showing the deep recess of the colonnade, providing a covered area that would be shaded for much of the day.

3.11
Pompeii. Plan of the
House of Faun showing
the sequence of spaces.
There is visual connection
from the street to the rear
garden.

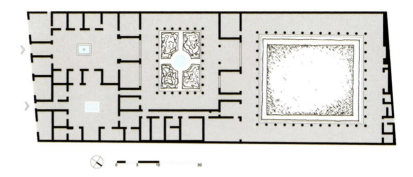

Water was used as an ornamental device in the form of a fountain, and as a pool lined with mosaic, and adorned with statuary. Running water would break the stillness of the courtyard, which in much of the Roman empire would have been hot and sultry in summer. Bushes were often clipped and shaped. Nature, having been shaped and controlled by the owners of the garden, was transformed. *Figure 3.11.*

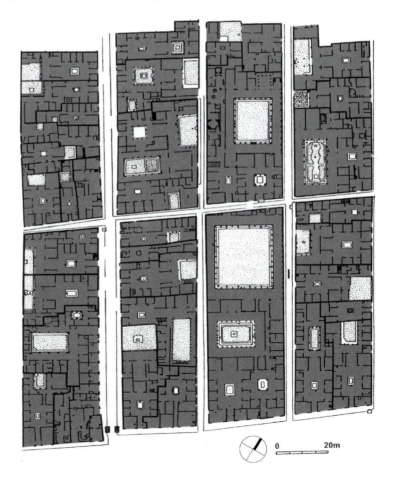

3.12
Plan of Pompeii indicating
a consistent pattern of
open spaces that go deep
into the plots.

Taming nature **77**

3.13
Aerial view of the town of
Pavia, Italy showing much
of the original Roman
layout.

Murals were often painted on a wall to create an illusion of more space, and compensate for cramped conditions. They introduced another theatrical layer to the space, where occupants could suspend disbelief and enter an imaginary world beyond their material surroundings. The murals might depict popular mythological scenes that were felt to be an appropriate narrative for the family, even an imaginary hunting park, a reference to pairidaeza.

It is clear that many gardens, even the most humble, aimed to be beautiful as well as utilitarian, and there is widespread evidence of designs that would stimulate and satisfy a desire to be close to nature, of aspirations to establish *rus in urbe,* an illusion of countryside in the town that transcended class and wealth. The garden was so integrated into the Roman way of life that the designs of house and garden could not be separated. The resulting type of dwelling was versatile enough to adapt to many different locations. It is a legacy of the Roman empire that other civilisations have adopted versions of the peristyle house with its enclosed garden. *Figure 3.13.*

Enclosed gardens in the Christian world

Hortus conclusus and the expression of a belief system

With the fading of the Roman empire, pragmatism in the layout of gardens and architecture gave way to new models. There was an increasing emphasis on the religious significance of the garden. It came to be seen as representing a closed world that required spatial separateness. It gave rise to the *hortus conclusus*[10] in the Christian world and the garden as expressions of Earthly Paradise in Islam.

> A garden enclosed is my sister, my spouse; a spring shut up. A fountain sealed.
>
> Thy plants are an orchard, of pomegranates, with pleasant fruits; camphire, with spikenard,
>
> Spikenard and saffron; calamus and cinnamon, with all trees of frankincense; myrrh and aloes, with all the chief spices:
>
> A fountain of gardens, a well of living waters, and streams from Lebanon.
>
> Awake O north wind; and come, thou south; blow upon my garden, that the spices thereof may flow out. Let my beloved come into his garden, and eat his pleasant fruits.[11]

The *hortus conclusus* is associated with the Virgin Mary and refers to this passage from the Song of Solomon in the Old Testament of the Bible. The closed garden, empty of people, represents the womb of her virginal state, as yet un-entered. Paintings of the late medieval period show that although she may be alone, she is surrounded by flowering plants, all of which have symbolic significance for the onlooker. For example, the white lily is a symbol of purity, red roses represent the blood of martyrs and violets are for the Virgin's humility.[12] *Figure 3.14.* The Virgin Mary herself was often described as a Paradise. Christ, the tree of life, lay at her centre within her womb. Paintings of the annunciation often depict her in a colonnaded space, located between the house and garden. The colonnade mediates between the two spaces, giving equal importance to both. They protect and contain her, and provide a safe location for her encounter with the Angel Gabriel, and an appropriate background for a moment of intimacy, which is often depicted in a very moving manner. *Figure 3.15.*

The medieval garden

The countryside and city were not relaxing places in medieval Western Europe. Much of the countryside was uncultivated, wild and unsafe. Cities were overcrowded and had no sanitation, their streets smelly, unpaved, noisy and chaotic. Enclosed gardens provided safe havens, calm and quiet breathing spaces. Very few of them survive, and consequently they have had less direct impact on subsequent garden design than those of their

Islamic counterparts.[13] Most of our knowledge comes from contemporary records, writings, paintings and engravings. Secular gardens can be seen within an enclosing building, wall or fence, described by John Harvey[14] as 'the horticultural chamber music of the time'.

3.14
The Little Garden of Paradise. Upper Rheinish Master *c.*1410. The painting depicts Mary seated on a turf bench, reading and listening to music. The trees of life and knowledge border the garden.

3.15
The Annunciation by Domenico Veneziana, 1442–48. The Angel Gabriel is located in a space open to the sky, whereas Mary is protected by the colonnade. The fertile garden behind provides another layer of protection and is symbolic of the Virgin birth.

Religious allegory thrived in the medieval period as a means of interpreting ideas of good and evil, heaven and hell. These were portrayed throughout the arts, and through architectural and garden design, particularly in religious houses. Despite their religious underpinning, many secular gardens were designed purely for pleasure. There is evidence to suggest that gardens would often contain a central fountain, with paths leading from it. The wall was essential, not only to keep out unwanted flora and fauna, but also to keep any pagan gods at bay that might still be lingering in the wilds of the countryside. We know that the designs were much influenced by the Roman occupation, and also by contact with the Middle East through pilgrimages, trading, the Crusades and the Moorish occupation of Spain.

During the thirteenth and fourteenth centuries a secular variant of the *hortus conclusus* became known through the tradition of courtly love. It is particularly well illustrated in the long poem, *Le Roman de la Rose*[15] which has inspired many illustrations. The poem describes the hero's quest

3.16

Lutenist and singers in garden. Illustration of the *Roman de la Rose*. Lady Idleness shows the Lover the door to the garden. Inside, there is an idyllic scene of a musician entertaining finely dressed women with his lute playing, and another man standing by to one side.

for a rose as the quest for his lady's love, and, in the first part of the poem, it takes place within a walled garden, where he is tutored in the art of courtship.[16] *Figure 3.16*. The *hortus delicarium*[17] depicted in the poem became the secular version of the *hortus conclusus*. Such poems inspired the designs of gardens for enjoyment, and escape, particularly for women of means. The components – enclosing wall, water, a fountain and perhaps a turf bench – are typical of many gardens of the period. They became known as Love Gardens, and were the refuges of writers, poets, or for philosophical thought as much as for courting couples and lovers. They were places where direct experience of the flowers and plants could be enjoyed, chosen for their scent, colour, foliage, textural quality as well as for their many appropriate symbolic references.

Islamic foundations

Metaphorical space and the Chahar Bagh

Although there is speculation over the designs of Roman and medieval European gardens, this is not the case in Islam. The hot dry conditions of their locations have helped preserve Islamic gardens. The Qur'an refers explicitly to Paradise as a garden, secluded and physically separate; a tangible place that corresponds to our own interior world. For artists and designers of the time, the representation of paradise required an imaginative transformation of ideas into reality. This was fuelled by the banning of all figurative imagery. The transformation took place by abstracting nature through mathematics and geometry. For mosques and seminaries it was not thought appropriate even to have a planted garden, as it could lead to the distraction of peoples' thoughts. As a consequence, much energy went into the design of the façades of the enclosing buildings, and the ground. Buildings were elaborately decorated with relief work, geometric patterning and calligraphy. Colour was added to the fabric of the buildings, particularly through the use of ceramic tiles. Paving and water were exploited over the ground surface, through decorative tiles, reflective pools, fountains and channels. *Figures 3.17, 3.18*.

Secular gardens flourished throughout the golden age of Islam from the Indian subcontinent across North Africa to the Iberian peninsular. The sacred and visionary, and the secular and hedonistic influenced each other and proved to be very creative.[18] The combination of the underlying mathematical layout, and an acceptance of the garden responding to the sensuous side of our natures, did not conflict with any religious and spiritual teachings as it did in Christianity. If Mohamed promoted the idea of Paradise as a reward for life of the faithful, it was fitting that gardens should reflect the idea of Earthly Paradise.[19] *Figure 3.19*.

The template for the garden as Earthly Paradise lies within the pure geometry of a square, and its division into four. There is a central fountain, usually flowing into a pool, and the water overflows into four channels that divide it into four equally sized smaller squares. The fountain, reaching up to heaven represents God on Earth, and the streams represent the four rivers of the world that divide up the four continents. This division also represents the four cardinal points, the four elements and the four seasons. It is best demonstrated in the Chahar Bagh,[20] which has come to be known

3.17
Medersa Ben Youssef Theological College, Marrakech. Fourteenth century, reconstructed in sixteenth century. The sides to the courtyard are elaborately decorated with caligraphy, coloured patterned glazed tiles and relief work based on detailed geometric patterns, carved into cedar, marble and stucco. There is no representation of plants and no planting in the courtyard.

as one of the blueprints of Islamic Paradise Gardens. It also serves as a basis for a repeating pattern that can be spread over larger areas. It can be scaled up and down with ease, and is easily divisible, creating smaller versions of the orthogonal pattern, using paths and water. This symbolic shape, representative of and distilled from descriptions within the Qur'an,

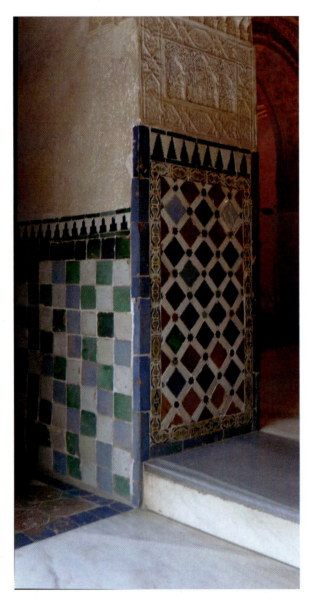

3.18
The Alhambra. Detail of threshold to one of the courts.

Taming nature

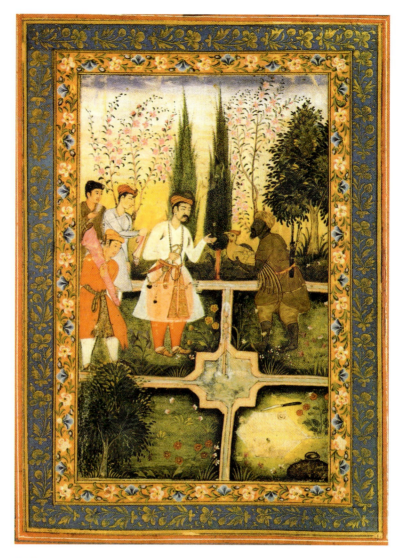

3.19
Prince (Babur) in a garden presented with a jungle-fowl, in a garden divided into
four with a central fountain and pool.

became a metaphor for the organisation and domestication of the
landscape.[21] *Figures 3.20, 3.21.*

The Chahar Bagh layout refers to the flat plane of the garden, but if
the space is enclosed, it is likely that the architecture will also respond to
the patterns, through the articulation of a façade and colonnade. Columns
also provide a framework for us to look into the garden, themselves a
representation of trees.

Taming nature

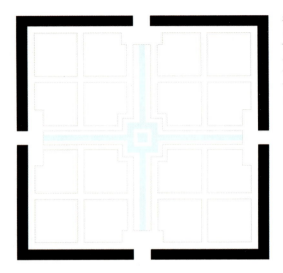

3.20
Plan of the basic layout of the Chahar Bagh, with a central fountain, pool and four channels flowing from them that divide the garden into four.

Earthly Paradise and the Alhambra

And by the garden channels were does,
hollow, pouring water,
sprinkling the plants in the garden beds . . .
and everything fragrant as spices,
everything seemed perfumed with myrrh.
    Birds were singing in the boughs,
peering through the fronds of palm,
and there were fresh and lovely blossoms-
roses, saffron, narcissus-
and each was boasting that he was best
(though we thought everyone was beautiful).
The narcissi said, 'We are so white
We rule the sun and moon and stars!'[22]

3.21
Paradise garden.

This fragment of a Hebrew poem by ibn Gabirol was written in medieval Spain, in a period of religious tolerance and cultural richness, at the time of Al Andalus, under Moorish occupation. It describes the Generalife Gardens that accompany the Nazrid Palaces of the Alhambra complex, strategically placed above the town of Granada in Spain, dominating the town and its hinterland. *Figure 3.22*. Together they are considered to be some of the finest examples of a fusion of landscape, architecture, courtyard and garden, where the notion of Earthly Paradise has been imaginatively embodied and continuously interpreted over many generations since the twelfth century. It was started when the boundaries between art and science, and the different disciplines of the arts we have today, did not exist. *Figures 3.23, 3.24*.

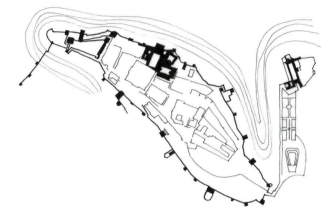

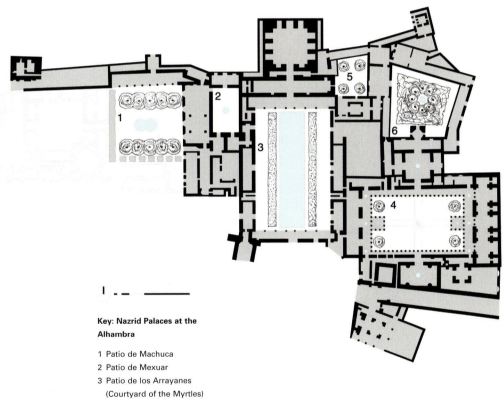

**Key: Nazrid Palaces at the
Alhambra**

1 Patio de Machuca
2 Patio de Mexuar
3 Patio de los Arrayanes
   (Courtyard of the Myrtles)
4 Patio de Los Leones
   (Courtyard of the Lions)
5 Patio de los Cypeses
6 Patio de Lindaraja

3.23
Plan of the Nazrid Palaces.

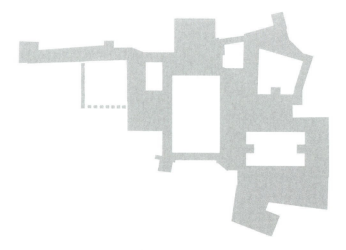

3.24
Simplified plan of Nazrid Palaces showing proportion and juxtaposition of internal and external space.

There are three main interconnected palaces, each with their own patios. Although they have been adapted to suit a Christian culture after the Moors had left, the basic layout has not been altered, and the patios are intact. Each is integral with the surrounding architecture and is deeply embedded within the complex. No attempt is made to create linear visual links between each other or the outside world. As you walk through it today, it is easy to feel disoriented by an apparent maze of staggered junctions, through layers of space that make up a complex choreographed sequence.[23] Planting in the patios is sparse. Water is plentiful, much of which runs from pools to rills, and in some cases penetrates far into the interior spaces. Each patio exhibits an extraordinary wealth of architectural virtuosity, where interior, exterior, sculpture, decoration, art and science all intertwine. The simplicity of the overall space of each patio is implicit through its pure cuboid geometry that holds all the other architectural moves together. Each has a unique character but is entirely integrated within the whole scheme.

The proportions of Mexuar Patio are relatively small and convincingly room-like. It has no plants at all, and only a single centrally-placed pool. As you approach it, the main façade of the Comares Palace shimmers in front of you, framed by the arches of a double-layered colonnaded anteroom. The highly decorated but smooth surface gives the appearance of an internal wall of a room, complementing the other two uninterrupted adjacent sides, which are now bare. A glimmer of light can be seen through two layers of façade and wall, the only indication of where to go next. *Figure 3.25.*

The Court of the Myrtles, Patio de los Arrayanes, is a grand space, dominated by the Comares Tower and a long, still, centrally placed rectilinear pool, proportioned to perfectly reflect the façades of the buildings. *Figure 3.26.* There is a small circular pool at both ends, each with a central fountain that represents birth and life. There is a long axial view, but access is around the edges. The smaller scale of the windows and doors along the flanking walls, and the planting provide a sense of human proportion within this awe-inspiring space. Nature is represented by two long clipped myrtle hedges that add an intermediary layer between building and water.

The Court of the Lions, Patio de los Leones, is intensely inward-looking and the most elaborate, containing a clear pattern of the Chahar Bagh, with its central fountain and rills that divide the floor into four. A complicated mathematical game is being played. You look through and across to a forest of slender columns that protrude into the space on all four sides

3.25
View across the Mexuar Patio toward the façade of the Comares Palace.

3.26
View of the Court of the
Myrtles, looking toward
the Comares Tower. The
low myrtle hedges line the
two long sides of the pool.
It is possible to see a
perfect mirror image of
the palace reflected in the
water.

to make little pavilions. *Figure 3.27*. Twelve carved stone lions surround
the central fountain. Water flows from their mouths into a collecting pool
and then into four channels that penetrate into the building, and end in small
circular pools each containing another fountain that gurgles pleasantly as
you pass. The channels of water in the patio represent agricultural control
over the land as well as to the Qur'an references.[24] The natural world is
restricted to four shaped citrus bushes in each corner.

The gardens to the north and east were built long after the Moors
had left. The further away from the main palaces, the more planting has a

3.27
The inward-looking Court of Lions is highly decorated, and seen initially through a forest of slender columns.

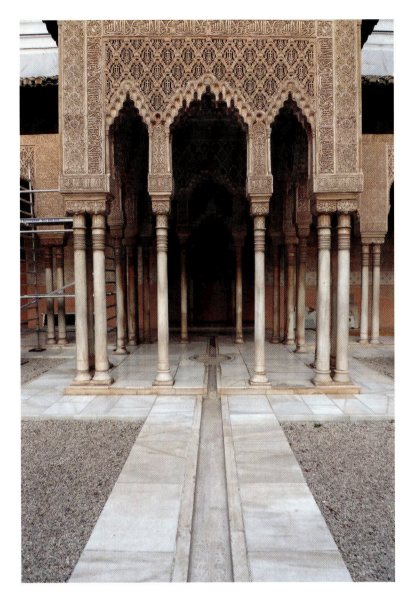

presence. The Patio de Lindaraja sits on the edge of the complex, a late addition, built to compensate for the lost view over Granada from the Lindaraja Mirador as the palace was extended and the view obscured. It submits to the landscape and is not rectilinear. Although the mathematical purity is lost, it manipulates the space and the level change without losing a sense of enclosure. The four square plan is maintained, but with much more planting. Box trees outline the geometric pattern; cypress and orange trees provide shade, colour and scent. The Partal Gardens are situated beside the complex, which together with the Partal Palace, have been

created over the ruins of the palace of the Count of Tendrilla, and designed
to be in the spirit of the original. They comprise a series of continuous garden
rooms, many variations on the theme of the Chahar Bagh. *Figure 3.28*. Water
runs through them, taking advantage of gravity on the sloping site, and the
basic patterns are repeated and reinvented. The paths are shaded with
pomegranate trees, the *granadas*.

     The Alhambra palace complex is an example of the possibilities open
to the rich and powerful, and where artistry has been valued. Each space
has its own integrity, and complements the interiors that surround it, through
proportion and attention to detail. The gardens range from being filled with
an abundance of plants, to their complete absence. Contrast and continuity
without visual connection between spaces make this an exceptional place.

The Islamic house

> The same magic floated among the infinite heights of the
> heavens and the small hollow of this perfect garden, the only
> reality visible on earth. The silence that filled it, made more
> poignant by the unique sound of water in the marble basin
> in the centre of the garden, seemed to descend from the
> celestial heights. There was an element of eternity from
> above that flowed into the perishable things here on earth.[25]
>
> André Chevrillon

The inclusion of the courtyard garden was not restricted to grand palaces,
and they can be found in almost all traditional Islamic houses even today.
Figures 3.29, 3.30. Although the main drivers of the design of houses are

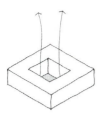

3.29
Views from within only up to the sky.

3.30
No direct view into the interior from the street.

responses to climate and social structure, the evocation of Earthly Paradise has also been important.

The layout of the traditional Arab courtyard town house of the Maghreb region of North Africa is introverted and concentric, and turns it back to the street. The domestic life of its inhabitants revolves around the courtyard. It is the women's domain, and it is their main contact with the natural world. Its spatial configuration has to resolve the conflicts of Islamic social boundaries, where the territories of men and women are clearly defined. Entry to the house is along a staggered route, avoiding any direct visual contact from the street to the courtyard. The courtyard usually has an imposed square geometry. It reconciles irregularities of the plot and provides a central focus for all domestic activities. The high walls provide shade in the heat of the day and the colonnade that surrounds it also provides shaded access to the rooms behind it. A central fountain is often present for its symbolic significance as much as for pleasure. *Figure 3.31.*

A particular type of courtyard house, the *riad* has developed in Morocco. Riad literally means a house that has been planned around a garden.[26] *Figure 3.32.* Riads in towns, such as the Medina area in Marrakech, are amassed and appear to be almost mounded together to form a tight-knit city network, and there is little leftover space for gardens. *Figure 3.33.* The most striking aspect of this town house is the contrast with its immediate surroundings. From the confined spaces of the *souk,*[27] with its covered streets that teem with people, donkeys, mopeds and cats; that are overloaded with merchandise ranging from carpets to hard boiled eggs; layered with colours and patterns; punctuated with strips of sunlight, filtered light, shade, smoke; thick with perfume, exhaust fumes, cooking smells

3.31
Dar Bouhellal in the Medina, Fez. The ground floor plan demonstrates a typical layout of an urban house, with a rectilinear courtyard set in an irregularly shaped plot that cannot be seen from the entrance.

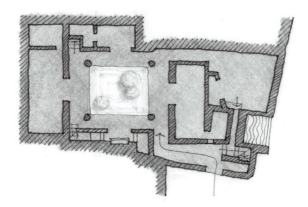

3.32
Riad (courtyard garden) in
Marrakech.

3.33
Aerial view of Marrakech
showing the organic
shape of the town, its
density and the regularity
of square-shaped
courtyard gardens in the
middle of each plot.

and drains; filled with a cacophony of noise emitted from all the activities, the lanes spread out to the residential areas. A warren of bare narrow streets tunnel their way through the town. Their walls often have a rough mud render finish with few openings, and doors are set discreetly within them. You go from chaos to calm as you enter and step into a blind corridor, walk toward the light and finally move into an orderly, light tranquil open space, a haven after the bustle of the *souk. Figures 3.34, 3.35.* Separate sounds can be distinguished: the trickle of water from a pool, or a person's footsteps in the background. Walls are often painted white, setting off the shape of a flowering bush, or the detailed pattern of some ceramic tiles. *Figures 3.36, 3.37.*

3.34
Marrakech. A street leading away from the souk.

3.35
Marrakech. Streets turn into tunnels, with occasional light shafts. Entrance doors are
discreetly set into the side walls.

3.36
Marrakech. Inside the riad the orderly square space, lit by a deep shaft of natural light, is the focus to the house. (Dar el Quadi)

Only if you climb the stairs to the rooftops can you observe the city, a series of broad flat rooftop terraces punctuated with a proliferation of satellite dishes and with square-shaped wells in the middle. Light-hungry greenery overflows out of them from the gardens below. It is here that we find openness, and unbounded views that stretch across to the High Atlas Mountains. *Figure 3.38.*

Taming nature

3.37
The plain white background of the building brings out the colour and texture of the planting.

3.38
Marrakech. The city opens
up at roof level. Plants
and trees can be seen
emerging from the
courtyard gardens below.

Cultural adaptability

The courtyard house, *the casa patio*, in Cordoba, Southern Spain has survived through hundreds of years of occupancy, from the Romans, to the Moors, through to Christian occupation, and is thriving today in a secularised society. During the Moorish occupancy the urban landscape had virtually no civic structure and ceased to adhere to the orthogonal Roman planning that had been based on a municipal organisational regime. Neighbourhoods developed into a fragmented but close-knit pattern, squeezed within the city walls and on top of the Roman foundations. Many of its narrow streets were accessible only on foot. As it converted to Christianity in the fifteenth and sixteenth centuries, the city opened up again and created more public spaces, many of which are still in place today.

Like Marrakech, the streets and external walls of the terraced houses are relatively plain, with the exception of the threshold to each house, which is celebrated with a decorated surround. The solid timber front doors are often open or kept ajar. It is possible to get a glimpse of first a passageway lined with decorative tiles that reflect light into the interior, and then deep into the middle of the house to the patio, a garden brilliantly lit and full of colour, that lies beyond an open-grilled door. *Figure 3.39.* There is likely to be a mixture of trees and shrubs planted directly into the ground, together with an abundance of potted plants. On larger plots it is common to have two patios. The one nearest the street is on display, whereas the second is more private, but not completely hidden. *Figure 3.40.* The stair often comes directly off the patio, leading to a gallery on the upper level. In most aspects the colonnaded courtyard garden adheres to the Islamic

3.39
Cordoba. Entrance to a
town house that has its
door kept ajar, allowing a
view through from the
street to a patio at the
rear.

urban house type. It is adopted as the central living space, and is a thorough-
fare to most rooms within the dwelling, both at ground level and above.
The roofs will frequently be pitched inwards, to collect the rainwater, a
reminder of the Roman impluvium. The visual connection to the patio from
the street also derives from Roman origins. The *reja* the open-grilled gate,
is an interesting development of the two cultures. It is usually closed and
locked, but as it is made of open decorative ironwork, it allows a view from
the street whilst maintaining security.

Adaptation for the twenty-first century

The *casa patio* continues to be used as a house type and has been adapted
to twenty-first-century needs. The layout can extend beyond the single
dwelling and used for apartments. There is a long history of the courtyard

3.40
Cordoba. The first more public courtyard leads through to a second more private one. The reja (grille) in the foreground will ensure security, but still allow the view through.

serving as a central space for multiple occupancy of a building. A derivation of the Roman *insula,* the first known block of flats, can be seen in Cordoba. Originally, large plots were often divided internally, either for members of an extended family or for small apartments, a housing type that Cordoba has continued to make use of. There are many infill sites within the old city structure where this type of house is used. The building is taken up to the boundary of the street, and access to the apartments is through a passage off the pavement, through a reja that is kept locked, and then into a shared patio. *Figure 3.41.*

In both Marrakech and Cordoba, houses based around a courtyard garden are actively used today. Their histories have been very varied, and

Taming nature

they have survived periods of both high and low status. Today their design has been reassessed, and their popularity is testament to their adaptability to contemporary life. The typology reflects responsiveness to climate conditions with the potential for very low energy consumption. It is anchored by the enclosed garden.

Through tracing the development of the enclosed garden in different periods in history, certain features have remained consistent, and have been able to be adapted to a range of climatic and cultural differences. The bounded open space of the courtyard garden has provided the focus for domestic activity or a site for action. Its longevity lies both in utility and in its metaphorical significance.

4 Ritual and emptiness –

and the rigour of developing an idea

Encounter

I first encountered the cloister of the Cistercian Monastery of Le Thoronet when I was studying architecture. It was one of our destinations on a field trip to the south of France. We had the good fortune to be shown around by the architectural historian François Cali,[1] and he not only gave us a very detailed analysis of the monastery and description of the daily life of the inhabitants in the twelfth century, but, on top of that, he managed to convey the emotional impact of this extraordinary building, and brought it to life as it might have been for the monks. I revisited it in the summer of 2009, finding it much altered since 1973 when it was all but derelict. It still had the same power, despite the touristification and much-needed renovation.

This time we descended from the car park through the woods to a gatehouse, and were ushered in through the ubiquitous shop and ticket office, and only then led through a landscape of grassy slopes and ruined walls toward the first of the abbey buildings, the Lay Brothers' quarters. We passed through an opening to the side of it into a courtyard. Ahead was the door to the cloister. We passed abruptly from light to dark, to light and to very dark. After a moment or two our eyes adjusted and we could see a cloistered space so deep and its walls so thick that it felt completely internal, and removed from the world. As we walked around the simple barrel-vaulted space, it was almost cave-like and gave the impression that it could have been carved out of one solid block. The stone glowed with a mixture of rich warm greys and yellow ochres. *Figures 4.1, 4.2.*

4.1
Le Thoronet. Looking across to the external wall of the cloister with the stone brilliantly lit by the Provençal sunlight.

4.2
Le Thoronet, looking at the external wall from within the cloister walkway. The sun coming through the openings creates pools of bright light.

The building, standing up to the ferocity of the sun, seemed to gently enfold and wrap itself around us as we moved through it and started our ascent to the church. Although the cloister garden was bare and the grass dried out, the space came alive through the architecture. The thoughts and feelings of the masons still seemed to be present. Even now, with the experience of an empty uninhabited building rather than that of a religious order, it is not difficult to imagine the time when it was inhabited. The simplicity of form, the fall of light and the unique shape of the cloister have given it a timeless quality. The use of one material, stone, so precisely cut, the simplicity of the unornamented openings and the proportioning that is both adjusting to the land and to the purpose of the cloister, give it an awe-inspiring power that makes Le Thoronet stand out as an exceptional building.

Metaphorical space

This chapter will look at the enclosed garden as an imagined place as well as a material space, a representation of ideas, a place for us to negotiate around, and contemplate, as much through absence as presence. It will look at the reciprocal relationship between the encircling architectural elements – wall or building – and the space itself. It will consider the garden as a condensation of nature, a distillation of ideas, where the design and the fabric of the surrounding building make a significant contribution to its presence. I will start by analysing two designs from the past that rely on an all-encompassing system of beliefs about life, conduct and the cosmos: Cistercian architecture and the enclosed Zen dry gardens of Japan. In both, the gardens are to be looked at, not inhabited, and lived in only in the mind. What can we gain from looking at them today in a secular society where conditions are very different? By analysing a twentieth-century building alongside them, I will discuss key features of the chosen examples that are not only expressions of a particular period, but through attention to site, location, context and the way materials are put together, transcend their particular beliefs and can still be valuable references for designers today.

Cistercian architecture and the importance of the cloister

Monastic background

In the late Middle Ages, with the growth of Christianity, there was an expansion of monasteries throughout Europe and the Mediterranean, and new ground was being broken in architectural design. There were clear guidelines to be followed for expressing the practice and beliefs of the religion. As we have seen in the monastery at Pavia, a layout developed that was generated from the two main spaces: church and cloister. One was for the act of worship, the church, and the other, the cloister garden – a representation of the Garden of Eden or Paradise – for the contemplation of spiritual matters and God.[2] A self-contained community needed many other rooms; somewhere to prepare food, eat communally, sleep, to heal the sick and to meet and discuss matters of the community. These were placed around the cloister garden, and connected by the cloister walk. Variation in local conditions could be accommodated, as could the architectural expression of a particular monastic order, such as Benedictine, Cistercian, or Carthusian. The monastic day was arranged around a balance between work and prayer. Hard work and self-denial were part of the way to Paradise, the reward for enduring our time on earth. Heaven had to be sought, as Hell was unthinkable: 'Paradise was an ever present and almost palpable cultural concept.'[3]

Despite the emphasis of Paradise being an imagined abstract space, we should not lose sight of the cloister as a material site. We have evidence in many cases of a garden divided into four segments with a fountain at the centre, representing a tangible connection with God, life-giving and life everlasting, and has some similarities to the Chahar Bagh. Planting flowers and shrubs was not considered necessary unless they were there as symbolic reminders, such as the cypress tree, rising up to heaven, and its association with death. The layout set the pattern for the outlying cloister gardens. Many, however, were often simply grassed.[4] Washing, both as an act of ritual cleansing, as well as keeping clean, took place here too, often in a small aedicular shelter, the *lavabo*, the one physical intrusion into the space.

The power of the cloister lies in its centrality. It would absorb the rhythms of the day. It was designed to be wide enough for monks to assemble, and to process together into the church for prayer. Instruction could also take place here, as well as more solitary activities such as reading of the scriptures. *Figure 4.3*. Through meditation and ritualised walking the space was transformed. Even now the cloister comes to life as we move around it. Its material presence is felt through the rhythm of footsteps complemented by the human scale of the open cloister wall that lets in a pattern of sunlight and shadows, throughout the day, connecting, but not giving direct access to the garden.

The programme for Cistercian architecture

By the twelfth century many monasteries had become very rich, and their buildings elaborately decorated and adorned. The rigour of a monk's life

4.3
One side of the cloister at Le Thoronet Abbey in Provence, France, has a bench which would originally have been used by monks for study and instruction and the ceremonial washing of feet. Nowadays it is a convenient place to instruct the tourists.

had vanished and had transformed into an existence of wealth, comfort and decadence. This made St Bernard, founder of the Cistercian Order, re-examine the Rule of St Benedict, the sixth-century founder of medieval monasticism, and reintroduce a very strict code of humility, obedience and poverty. A life was to be based on a balance between work and prayer. In his teaching and writing St Bernard talks of the first desert monks in Egypt, hermits in the wilderness. From his description, a generic plan was drawn up and a new architecture emerged, virtually stripped bare of decoration. Its success can be measured by the fact that the arrangement lasted for four centuries. *Figures 4.4, 4.5.* Certain remote areas across Europe, then

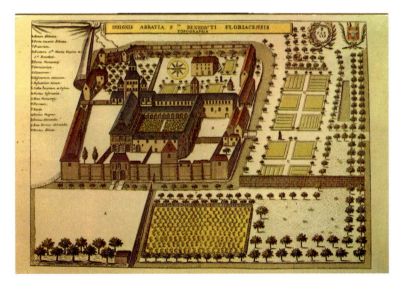

4.4
St Benoit sur Loire. Drawing showing the expansion of gardens that have grown around the central cloister.

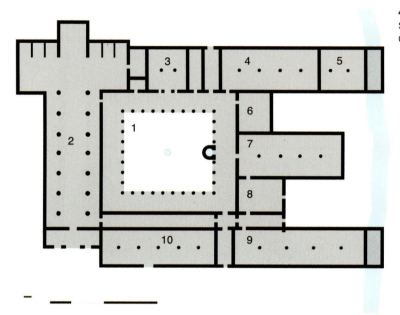

Key: Ideal Cistercian Layout

1 Cloister
2 Church
3 Chapter house
4 Monks' common room
5 Room for novices
6 Warming room
7 Refectory
8 Kitchen
9 Lay brothers' refectory
10 Cellar/store

considered to be a wilderness, were thought suitable locations for monks to escape from urban life and to collectively become hermits. Buildings had to be strictly functional and address the primary needs of the community. They had to be instruments for agricultural production, and accommodate rigorous religious rituals.

The task of the master masons was to create buildings and spaces that harmoniously reflected the Rule. There was to be no adornment, and no bright colours. The aesthetic would come out of the purity of the forms through the spaces created and the play of light. The carving of the stone was intended to bring out its intrinsic qualities. This could almost be a manifesto for the mid-twentieth century. The harmony of the building itself contributed to the internalising and strengthening of the monks' faith. As Wolfgang Braunfels shrewdly points out, with the denial of all figurative work and colour, all the artistry seems to have been poured direct into the architecture and thereby reached astonishing heights. [5] From strict adherence to the Rule, the most subtle and moving architectural sequences have been designed, using one material, stone, to manipulate light, sound and landscape.

Le Thoronet

Father Couturier, the instigator of one of Le Corbusier's most celebrated projects, La Tourette,[6] urged the architect to visit Le Thoronet before designing the new monastery. To Couturier it had the essence of what a

4.6
Central enclosed space.

4.7
Circulation around main space.

monastery should be, 'dedicated to monastic silence, meditation and devotion'.[7] An almost mystical quality has been achieved in Le Thoronet not only through material form and space, but through material form and *action*. The quality of the building can only be fully appreciated by us moving through the spaces. It was originally also dependent on ritual and silence, and the interpretation of the rules imposed by the Cistercians, to consider the problems of the individual maintaining his solitude within the community. *Figures 4.6, 4.7.*

Working with the land

The site for the new building at Le Thoronet in the south of France was chosen to be in the forest, but near to a stream and a spring, and where the land was known to be fertile. *Figures 4.8, 4.9, 4.10.* It slopes gently, and the masons responded with small adjustments to the generic plan. The impression one gets as a visitor, is that the monastery has yielded to the landscape, and buildings appear to grow out of it.

4.8
Le Thoronet. The monastery is still surrounded by dense forest.

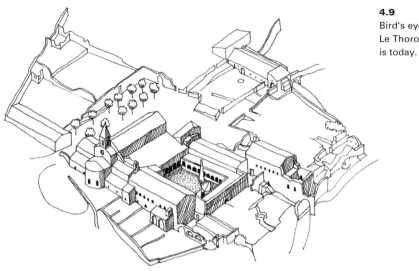

4.9
Bird's eye view of
Le Thoronet as it
is today.

4.10
Le Thoronet. Looking
across the cloister from
the upper level.

The first act of transgression was to invert the layout of the plan, placing the cloister and its related rooms to the north of the church. It gave easy access to the stream and placed the church at the highest point. Then, unlike most other monasteries, the cloister was made to be irregular in plan. A possible explanation is that the first building on site was the cellier,[8] which responded to the lie of the land, and despite these utilitarian considerations, by the time the church was built it was aligned exactly on the east–west axis, just 6.5° away from being at right angles to the cellier. This sets up two rectilinear grids, and the differences between the two geometries have been resolved within the cloister. *Figures 4.11, 4.12, 4.13.*

The cloister accommodates the natural slope of the site by mediating between all the rooms that have been necessarily located at different levels. With a level change of approximately three metres between the north and the south cloisters, the master masons resolved the difference by creating a ramped floor to the east and west cloister combined with steps near the approach to the church. *Figures 4.14, 4.15.* The steps not only serve their

Ritual and emptiness

4.11
Le Thoronet. General
arrangement.

Key: Le Thoronet

1 Church
2 Cloister
3 Chapter house
4 Lavabo
5 Cellar
6 Lay brothers

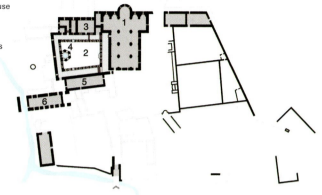

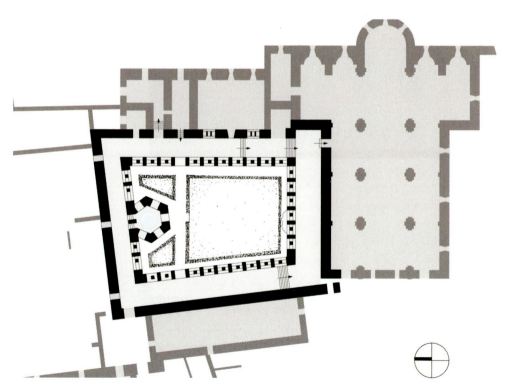

4.12
Le Thoronet cloister.

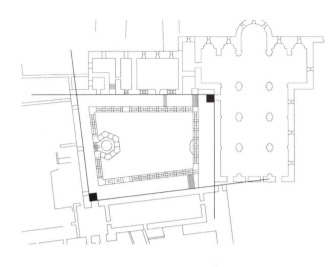

4.13
Diagram of geometry
of cloister. There is much
speculation about why the
cloister is not an exact
golden rectangle, and has
a discrepancy of 6.5° on
two sides.

4.14
Le Thoronet. Steps leading
up to the entrance to the
church.

4.15
Section through the cloister showing the difference in level between the lower and upper cloisters.

Ritual and emptiness

4.16
Rock appears in several parts of the monastery: in the cloister, the chapter house and inside the cloister near the church.

purpose of taking you up the slope, but also of altering your pace, and, in effect, adding to the drama of entry to the church, the most sacred space. The garden and cloister include lumps of raw rock left consciously bare that provide symbolic reference to the earth's crust. Rock is one of the rude elements of nature that provided caves for the first monks in the desert. *Figure 4.16*. In French, rock is *pierre*; and is a reference to St Peter, the rock, founder of the Christian Church.

The repeating arches of the cloister, providing an underlying visual framework, as well as a structural system, is regulated with the consistency of horizontal levels of the vaulted ceilings, the lower plinths and the cills of the openings into the cloister garden. Human scale, intensely felt throughout the whole monastery, is exemplified by the cloister. As you walk through you are conscious of the consistency of stark undecorated solid walls to one side and the rhythmical pattern of the uncommonly thick, arcaded walls that separate walkway from garden. The density of the walls is probably derived from the need to support the weight of an upper level cloister adjacent to the dormitory, but this cannot be the whole story. It is the well-judged proportion of what must be deliberately oversized masonry that gives it its magic.

Stone and sunlight

Stone was used in preference to wood as it is suggestive of permanence. Truth to materials was of great importance. The stone's essential qualities can be seen through the way sunlight falls on the different layering of the cloister wall and by the shadows it casts. It glows in the Provençal light, and radiates warmth. *Figure 4.17.* Today there is little evidence of the original cloister garden. All we have left is the rock, and the lavabo, and articulation

4.17
The warmth of the precisely cut limestone used throughout Le Thoronet is brought out by the sunlight.

of the cloister wall, a place that still captivates us. The openings are uniquely proportioned,[9] both in relation to the garden as a whole and to the vaulted walkway. *Figure 4.18*. Their depth gives them the appearance of small alcoves rather than window openings in a wall (approx. 1200mm). Their lack of ornamentation also gives a sculptural quality. Sunlight passing through them not only emphasizes the colouring of the stone, but also changes the feel of each walkway throughout the day. The stone stays warm long into the evening after the sun has set. Where the floor is ramped, the level cills of the openings apparently vary in height as the floor level rises or diminishes, and they suggest a range of places to sit, to lean against, or place a book. *Figure 4.19*.

4.18
The openings in the cloister wall are exceptionally deep compared with the size and proportion of the rest of the cloister, to the extent that they become spaces in themselves.

In the morning there is a strong alternating pattern of sunlight that stretches through the openings on the west side. As the day progresses they diminish and reappear on the east until the sun goes down in the west. *Figure 4.20.* This would have acted as a marker of time for the monks as they carried out their ritualised activities, always referring to the cloister, from early-morning prayer through to the evening when they would be reunited after their labours and process up to the church for prayer.

The dry gardens of Japan

Not clouded
mountains around the sea
in which I see the moon
the islands, become
holes in the ice

Saygio[10]

Background

The enclosed Zen dry gardens of Japan express a very different relationship with nature, based on reduction and distillation. Like the Cistercians, Zen monks had no respect for representational images as a means of artistic expression, but the art of the garden was acknowledged as being a fundamental expression of their beliefs. One of the significant ways to attain enlightenment, their ultimate goal, is through 'the mediation of natural phenomena'.[11] If we can reduce nature to its basic elements we can find a way to reach its essence, distilling it to its simplest expression, and hence regain our own original nature. By stripping the garden down to its barest elements, even draining it of water, we are left with the rock, and a quality of timelessness that takes us beyond our own temporal world. The context of Japanese Zen gardens starts with the myths that have built up around the unique landscape of Japan, where the entire natural world is animate, mountains and sea as well as trees and bushes. It is believed that contemplation of nature and natural phenomena is necessary to attain enlightenment. No distinction is made between the animate and inanimate, hence, in many cases rocks constitute a major part of the garden designs.

The Garden of Ryoan-ji

The small space adjacent to the Ryoan-ji Temple in Kyoto, dating back to the fifteenth century, is considered to be one of the finest examples of a Zen dry garden. The Ryoan-ji garden relies on suggestion, using nothing more than a few stones, a little moss and a gravel floor. It is enclosed by two wings of the temple complex and two free-standing low walls. *Figures 4.22, 4.23.* The garden itself is composed of 15 small rocks arranged in five groups surrounded by islands of moss within a sheet of meticulously raked light grey luminous quartzite. These highly symbolic rocks are positioned so that one rock remains hidden from view wherever you are placed on the veranda. A thin rectilinear frame of cut stone borders the garden and keeps the gravel in place, giving it a precise edge. The garden

4.21
Enclosed space in corner.

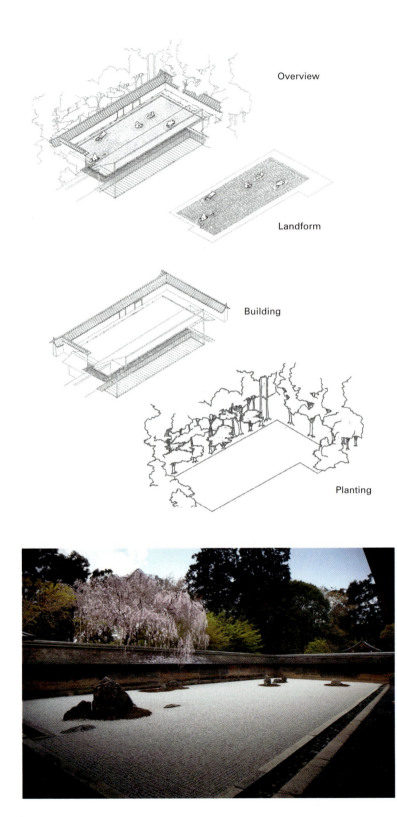

Overview

Landform

Building

Planting

4.22
Ryoan-ji, Kyoto, Japan.
Diagrammatic analysis
indicating the four major
components.

4.23
Ryoan-ji. View across the
dry garden.

is set within a band of pebbles on the temple side, reflective, darker and contrasting with the cut stone. The band of pebbles acts as a trough to collect any excess water run-off from the garden, and reduces the risk of flooding. It contributes to the appearance of elevating the horizontal plane of the garden, setting it apart and celebrating it. *Figure 4.24.*

The edge beside the free-standing walls is raised slightly, and finished with more roughly cut stone that also forms a narrow path that runs along the length of the wall. The wall itself is rendered in mud that

4.24
Ryoan-ji. Detail of boundary wall in spring.

had originally been boiled in oil. Over time the oil has leached out giving a richly textured patina of grey and black on top of the faded orange/yellow glow of the mud. It has a protective capping of shingles that also covers the path. On the temple side the transition from garden to interior is layered. Beyond the pebbles is a tiled walkway, and the floor of a timber veranda floats over it and mediates between interior and exterior. The veranda is meticulously articulated, crafted and positioned so that the garden can be observed directly from it. The overhang provides physical protection from the rain and sun, and its underside provides an upper frame to the view, dark against the daylight outside, leaving a sliver of sky, and emphasising the view downwards and across. The enclosing wall makes a clear visual separation between the garden and the external world, but does not attempt to conceal the view above it as much as it would in a cloister. The view of the landscape and trees that lie beyond the wall completes the composition, and the contrast between the external world and this abstract internalised one is extreme and provocative.

The walls and the framing set the garden apart and draw us in at the same time. There is nothing special about any one part, but the composition of the whole, of balance and asymmetry, of the juxtaposition of the weathered rocks and moss, set against the ephemeral perfection of the gravel, has not been surpassed. The result is enigmatic because we can see it as a microcosm of nature, as ranges of mountains rising from forested islands, surrounded by the sea, and we can also see it for what it is, or what is not there. No one enters a Zen garden, with the one exception of the priest whose task is to rake the gravel. The raking into meticulous patterns has an aesthetic function, but is also an act of contemplation for the monk.

There is no record of the designers' original intention and there is no single interpretation. François Berthier surmises: 'It is precisely because the significance of this garden remains vague that it is so rich in meaning.'[12] One of the attractions of places such as Ryoan-ji must be the way the designers have distilled the gardens, making large spaces unnecessary, suggesting that a whole landscape can be reduced to this small contained area. Ryoan-ji is about the size of a tennis court, and contains the universe.[13]

Layers of nature

The temple at Shoden-ji was first established in the thirteenth century. *Figure 4.25.* Its dry garden comprises a composition of large, rounded, very severely trimmed azalea bushes, grouped in clusters of three, five and seven. The trimming of them is so extreme that it has altered the pattern of their natural growth to the extent that the species is unrecognisable. These are living bushes, but they have also been transformed into abstractions of nature. They could be clouds, or mountains. They sit on top

4.25
Shoden-ji, showing the garden in the foreground, the trees behind it in the middleground and the mountain in the background that make up the whole composition.

of a sea of gravel that has been precisely raked into straight lines. The garden is surrounded on three sides by a plain white rendered rectilinear boundary wall, neatly capped with tiles, which, like the gravel, offsets the dark curved shapes within it. The garden, however, is in effect only the foreground of the full picture. The land directly behind it adds another important dimension. Your eye is taken up over the low wall and across a landscape full of mature trees such as cryptomerias and acers that forms an approximate v-shape. This middleground leads your eye through the cleft to a distant view of the sacred mountain Mount Hiei-zan in the background. This little garden captures an entire landscape. A technique has been used to capture a landscape 'alive' that is said to have its origins in the observation of the ink and wash drawings of landscape of the Chinese Sung Dynasty. The drawings often contained very small figures and buildings in the foreground, with a middleground, often deliberately vague and full of suggestion, that connected them to the grandeur of the mountain scenery in the distance.

Framing the view

In the late fifteenth century there was a proliferation of small Zen temples in Japan. A new architecture developed, that included a *shoin*, a reading room or salon, where works of art could be displayed, and literature discussed. The temples were often small, built as a private residence for a Zen priest, and on restricted plots of land that limited the size of the garden. One of the walls of the shoin would slide open to reveal a view of the garden.

This can be seen at Nanzen-ji Temple,[14] Kyoto. Sliding *shoji*[15] screens open out to provide a framed view on to the dry garden (called

Toranokowatashi – young tigers crossing the water). The garden is the foreground of a wider view of a landscape of trees, hillside and mountains. Whereas the view from the veranda is framed horizontally, the sliding shoji screens provide a vertical frame to the view from the shoin to the garden to complete the picture. *Figures 4.26, 4.27, 4.28.*

The translucent patterned screens also enable muted light to come through into the interior, even when they are closed. The continuous

4.26
Nanzen-ji. Looking out to the Hojo Garden from the salon/study.

4.27
Nanzen-ji. Detail of sliding screens.

4.28
Nanzen-ji. Detail of rock
and raked sand.

reflective polished timber floor leads your eye to the outside across the veranda to the garden. Veranda, corridor and screens give a complex layering of space between the interior and exterior, subtly connecting building, garden and landscape.

What could Cistercian cloisters and Zen temple gardens have in common, apart from the physical enclosure of the land? Although they appear to have no direct resemblance to Cistercian monastery gardens and, indeed, look very different, there are parallels that can be drawn. In both building types we are not invited and physically excluded from entering into the garden. Neither contain any decorative planting. The cloister and veranda are both transitional zones that spatially negotiate between the interior and the garden, and are wide enough to be inhabited and enable ritualised activities. Although the configuration of Le Thoronet and Ryoan-ji is different, the gardens are equally significant and important. We can walk around them, or sit beside them, but the experience is through the mind, through the act of looking and contemplating. Both of them have been built with a profound understanding of the materials used, whether it is the stone at Le Thoronet, or the slightly larger pallet of stones, moss and timber at Ryoan-ji. The edge condition of each is clearly defined, through the cloister wall, the veranda or the framing of the garden. Both are clearly structured, and representative of a greater dimension of time than the annual changing of the seasons.

Modern interpretation

Fondazione Querini Stampalia

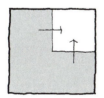

4.29
Views to a corner garden.

The renovation of the Fondazione Querini Stampalia in 1961–63[16] in Venice by Carlo Scarpa embodies certain similar aspirations to Le Thoronet and Ryoan-ji. It can be seen in the thoroughness and integrity of Scarpa's design, of his way of manipulating materials, structure and space, and the emphasis he has placed on the garden. He has acknowledged patterns of the past, and transformed them into a twentieth-century context. The Foundation is an old Venetian palace. Scarpa was commissioned to renovate and convert it into an art gallery and library. *Figure 4.30.* As part of the renovation Scarpa transformed the neglected courtyard into a garden, and integrated it with the internal exhibition spaces in such a way that we experience it as another room. Scarpa sets up a dialogue between city and garden, through the play of light on surfaces, water, and directed views into the garden.[17] The result is a reinterpretation of a traditional Venetian garden as well as an interpretation of Venice itself. Ideas and memories have been distilled into a garden in the heart of Venice, with the old and the new comfortably coexisting.

The garden is enclosed by two of the external walls of the museum building, and two high free-standing boundary walls that back onto narrow streets. The height of the walls relative to the length and breadth of the floor give the impression of a room-like space. They give a sense of enclosure, and the restricted view is inward looking, or upwards and across the Venetian skyline. Glimpses of the garden can be seen as you walk around and up through the exhibition, and hence it becomes a reference point. *Figure 4.31.*

As you walk from the exhibition space toward the garden, the separation of interior and exterior is mediated by the continuity of the floor material together with the use of large panels of glass. *Figure 4.32.* When you walk out into the garden you are faced with a lawn raised above ground level. Its height seems to elevate its status, and accentuates it as a horizontal plane. It is part of a continuous sequence of planes contained within the building that have been negotiated as you progress from street, over water and across interior surfaces. As the lawn is raised it prevents you from

4.30
Querini Stampalia
Foundation, Venice.
Looking down to the
garden from the first floor,
and across to Venice as
the backdrop beyond the
boundary walls.

4.31
Querini Stampalia
Foundation. Plan of
garden.

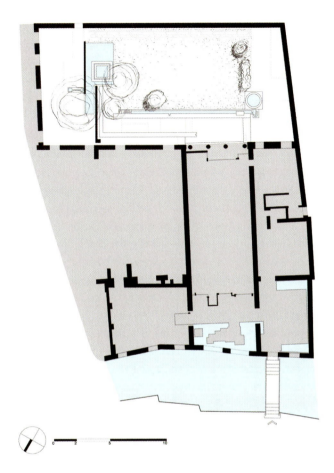

4.32
Querini Stampalia
Foundation. Approach to
the garden.

walking directly onto it. A low concrete wall containing a linear complex of water rills and sculptural pools runs along its length, reinforcing the framing and separation of the lawn. Together they provide a clear horizontal datum level, a constant around which your movements are choreographed. The sounds of Venice are present in the background, but you are more aware of the sound of water coming from the garden.

Your gaze is drawn diagonally across to the left toward a screen wall. It replaces an earlier nineteenth-century colonnade, and was originally designed by Scarpa to hide parts of the servicing areas of the Foundation. The grey concrete, with a rough shuttered finish, contrasts with the warm Venetian colours of old brick and stucco-work of the palazzo. There is a short run of bright and richly coloured Murano glass tiles inlaid within the rough concrete that shines out like jewellery, a reminder of the richness of materials used all over Venice.[18] You are invited to walk toward the screen, enticed by the stepped stone paving to the left, and then led around to a water lily pool, itself surrounded by a shallow water tray, where the journey terminates. *Figures 4.33, 4.34.*

If you turn right as you come out of the building, you climb some steep steps, past an old well, now dry, walk alongside one of the free-standing walls, and you reach the level of the lawn. The journey continues across stepping-stones laid in the grass (*Figure 4.35*) up to the screen. Only at this point can you pass though the screen to the smaller part of the garden which is now an outdoor extension to the café. When you first step out into the garden the screen appears to be a flat wall. When you come closer,

4.33
Querini Stampalia Foundation. Looking toward the screen.

Ritual and emptiness

4.34
Querini Stampalia
Foundation. Looking back
to the entrance from the
shallow reflecting pools.

4.35
Querini Stampalia
Foundation. The screen.

you realise that not only does it have openings, it is three-dimensional. It creates width and space through the bending of a single plane, making a three-dimensionally staggered zone that both connects and disconnects the two garden spaces.

From above, an implied circular route can be seen along all four sides of the main garden. The planting, although sparse, is now well established, filling much of the space and is in danger of interrupting the calm of the lawn that anchors it. *Figure 4.36.* Water is embraced throughout the scheme. Richard Murphy[19] observes that the Venetians are as obsessed by water as the British are with weather. Water is placed along a whole side of the lawn, and crafted into a series of miniature rills, waterfalls and pools, representing Venice and its waterways. The pools by the screen wall comprise a 'watery world floating in a shallow sea'.[20] This can be interpreted as Venice sitting precariously within the shallows of the Adriatic. The small sculptural maze of water at one end of the water sequence is reminiscent of both Venice, and of the Querini Stampalia itself. *Figures 4.37, 4.38.*

Many aspects of the design are resolved within this small area. Within this small space Scarpa provides us with a mixture of old and new, rough and smooth, dull and sparkling, still and moving. As Anne-Catrin Schultz says: 'The intentional treatment of materials, the deliberate use of the

4.36
Querini Stampalia Foundation. The path around the garden is completed with stepping-stones inserted into the grass.

4.37
Querini Stampalia
Foundation. Detail of
marble sculpture at one
end of the long water
channel.

4.38
Querini Stampalia
Foundation. Water spout
at the west end of the
water channel.

effects of light, and shadow, the poeticising of and symbolic functioning of
spaces and elements are commonalties that have to do primarily with an
attitude of mind.'[21] Scarpa's historical knowledge of Venice, together with
individual memories and experiences are woven together and reinterpreted
into his designs.[22]

Ritual and emptiness

The Foundation is secular and does not project any of the beliefs comparable to the earlier architecture discussed in this chapter. Nevertheless there are aspects that draw from the traditions represented by Le Thoronet and Ryoan-ji that equally apply to the Querini Stampalia. All three rely on a central flat plane that acts as a datum to hold together the built elements surrounding them. The datum is a point of stasis, a place to fix our gaze. They all express a condensation of ideas, expressed directly through both the architecture and the garden, whether, for example, it is by the simplicity of the cloister, the sea of gravel, or the folding wall. They all are designed to make use of the inherent qualities of the materials used, whether they are cut stone, rock, or concrete. All of the schemes have considered the users, and how they negotiate in and around the spaces, not just at a functional level, but as an experience. Water, or the representation of water, is a consideration in all three. Scarpa, through the meticulous refining of his design and his understanding of the spirit of the place, has managed to create an environment that transcends the ephemeral and reaches some of the timeless qualities embedded in the older buildings and gardens.

5 Sensory seclusion

The affective garden, the garden room as a scene for living

In search of the sensuous

My travelling companion and I were touring southern Portugal. It was the height of the tourist season and we were struggling to find a place to stay for the night that was affordable and away from the heart of the tourist strip. It was hot, we were tired, thirsty, and had been in the car for too long. We stumbled across a small sign on the roadside advertising a hotel. At last we were in luck. It turned out to be a magnificent converted sixteenth-century Quinta (country house). They had rooms for just that night. We were ushered into a courtyard and afternoon tea arrived on an elegant tray with some fine biscuits. We felt like royalty, or at least important diplomats. We sat in the shade, taking ownership of this beautiful, quiet place. We sipped our tea to the musical sounds of the fountain in front of us and a cool breeze brushed across our overheated brows. Tea had never tasted so delicious.

We were on our way to visit the Quinta da Bacalhoa, near Setubal in southern Portugal, famous for its garden. We arrived to find a flurry of gardeners, rotavators and large notices telling us that it was not open to the public. Several years passed before I was able to return. I was at a conference in Lisbon and had a few hours to spare. Although there was scant information on the website, I had to try again to visit the garden, taking a long bus ride out to the Azeitão district south of Lisbon, but it was like being in the film *Groundhog Day*.[1] The property was closed for renovation. This time I was bolder, and entered the garden through a rear entrance. A very polite head gardener told me to come back in a month's time. This short visit just gave me enough time to see that the estate and garden were indeed very fine. House, pavilions, garden and vineyard all had a very harmonious relationship with the underlying natural landscape.

My desire to visit the Quinta da Bacalhoa had been fuelled by the very colourful descriptions I had read.[2] *Figure 5.1.* The estate was conceived in the sixteenth century by Braz da Albuquerque, the son of Alfonso, the better known mariner and Viceroy of India. Braz was a much-travelled man, and had been particularly influenced by his trips to Italy and India, which can be seen reflected in the garden and the architecture. With its open-air loggias, walkways and seats, the garden was conceived as a place to enjoy both by looking at it, and through experiencing it. A stone perimeter wall encloses both the garden and a vineyard. Small pavilions are strategically placed along the wall that mediate between the level changes across the

5.1
View of Quinta da Bacalhoa, Portugal, showing characteristic lotus roof of the tower.

site. The estate, like a Palladian villa in the Veneto, integrates the family home with the farm. A square geometry is exploited throughout the design. *Figures 5.2, 5.3*. The L-shaped building makes up two sides of a square, and is placed to be in command of the whole site. A loggia looks directly onto a small square parterre, and then across a sunken citrus grove toward a square-shaped pool at the far end of the property. The view to the right looks across to the rest of the enclosure which is filled with vines. At first glance the parterre, with a sparkling fountain at its centre, appears to be wholly Italianate with its intertwined arabesques. *Figure 5.4*. Records suggest however that there was also a wall separating it from the tangerine grove that would have cut off the view. This discontinuity of space would appear to be more Moorish than Italian.[3]

As you walk down the path beside the hedge heading away from the parterre, the tank[4] comes into view, gleaming in the distance, and, according to the description, stimulates all your senses. It has now been replanted and will hopefully be returned to its former glory. The colours and the scent of the original planting would have been spectacular in contrast to the consistent green of the parterre. The heavy scent of tangerine blossom would be taken on the wind up onto the path, or you'd gaze at the bright orange of the fruits, contrasting with the glossy green leaves. The ground beneath was planted with silvery-blue leaved kale and artichokes, set against the dark red soil. The anticipation of the pleasure of eating the artichokes, peeling the leaves off slowly and eating the succulent flesh at the end of each leaf would complete the saturation of our senses. The path widens alongside the grove, suggesting a slower pace. This part

5.2
Quinta da Bacalhoa.
Plan of gardens.

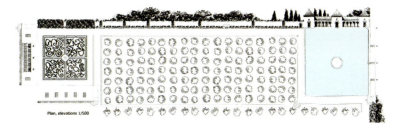

5.3
Diagrammatic section through one of the pavilions that negotiate three changes of level on the site.

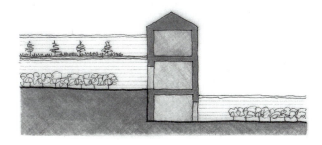

5.4
Quinta da Bacalhoa.
Looking over the parterre
to the loggia.

of the promenade was designed specifically for discussion and philosophical debate, where Braz and his friends and family could converse and consider matters of state (and the condition of the grapes). The tank at the end of the walk is lined with three small pavilions. Each is square in plan, and lined with fine decorative tiles, azulejos. The pavilions have deliberately been designed with small doors to exaggerate the size and grandeur of the ensemble. *Figure 5.5*. They provide shaded enclosures for people to sit in,

5.5
Quinta da Bacalhoa.
Looking toward the
pavilions in front of the
pool with the vineyards to
the left.

enjoy the shimmering reflection of the water on the tiles, or contemplate a little boat ride across the water. Although the tank is decorative, it serves as a reservoir for irrigating the farm. The path continues around much of the perimeter of the estate at a constant high level, whilst the land drops away, punctuated by the small pavilions.

I'm looking forward to my next trip.

Sensory experience

This chapter will focus on our sensory participation in the enclosed garden. The sensory garden exists for pleasure and participation, and for appreciation through corporeal engagement, whether it has been designed for enjoyment, therapy or spiritual well-being. An enclosed garden, through its inward-looking nature and adaptability in a range of climatic conditions, can have the effect of intensifying the atmosphere, and indulging our senses. In the book *Questions of Perception* [5] Steven Holl discusses how we are now very attuned to cinematic awareness, and film's power to convey atmosphere, through sound and the camera's eye. Even so we cannot smell a place shown on the screen, as equally we cannot feel the eddying wind, feel the texture of a weathered wall, or smell the intense odour of a newly mown lawn. Enclosure enhances our sensibilities by eliminating other distractions and literally *captures* the atmosphere. The lack of visual freedom created by boundary walls heightens perception through our other senses, liberating us from overemphasis on sight. Such controlled conditions can intensify our sensual responses and define its sense of place, its *genius loci.*

The senses

Listening, touching, smelling

The configuration of space created by an enclosing wall affects its micro-climate so that, for instance, a blustering wind can be replaced by stillness and encourage a sense of calm. The solid mass of enclosing walls can selectively eliminate much of the soundscape of the outside world, thus creating a space to fill with sounds, such as the particular ring and rhythm that footsteps make in a stone-paved colonnade as the sound bounces off the wall. Enclosure enables conversations to be held without having to raise voices, or for us to listen to the song of a blackbird, the trickle of water, or the sound of silence. *Figure 5.6.* As one is never very far away from the surroundings in an enclosed space, whether they are parts of the building or the plants, their textural quality affects us. Their closeness provokes us

5.6
Reflecting pool in the
Partal Gardens, Alhambra,
Spain.

to touch and feel. Juhani Pallasmaa, talking of the importance of touch, suggests that touch can be said to have a shape, because through touch and texture we understand weight, density and temperature.[6] *Figure 5.7.*

We are aware of the materiality of an enclosed garden through its accessibility. Contact with smoothness of a well-worn oak bench, the texture of a weathered wall, a stone seat warmed by the sun, or the softness of

5.7
Querini Stampalia garden.
Cool water on a hot day.

a lawn are appreciated through touch. *Figure 5.8.* But touch goes beyond immediate body contact with our environment. Temperature as well as texture is felt through our skin and the outer layers of our bodies. In temperate climates, dampness causes a sensation that we feel through our skin. If a lot of shade is created, damp corners can persist and have a negative effect on us. Similarly, dryness can be difficult to tolerate in hotter climates if there is little humidity.

Pallasmaa also talks of the 'space of scent'.[7] Enclosure can be an olfactory container of smells, an olfactory chamber. This is a good thing if the smells are pleasing, but more of a problem if the dead leaves from the

5.8
Wall constructed from recycled materials – brick and stone – creating texture and colours.

autumn have not been cleared away and started to rot. Dampness can be detected through smell as well as being felt through the skin, and the heat of the sun warming a space promotes the release of scents from plants. The memory of the scent of a flower can last long after the flower has withered. The memory of a particular past experience can be triggered by rediscovering that same smell many years after the event. Although this phenomenon works equally with both good and bad smells, there can be a thrill of walking out of a door into an enclosed garden not only to be greeted by the heat and brightness of the sun, but to be saturated in the heavy scent of honeysuckle that provokes a memory of a past event.

Looking and seeing

For most of us, hearing, smelling and touching are perceived within the context of what we see. The design of enclosed gardens inevitably relies on what can be seen and how it can be viewed. An enclosed garden can be seen as a stage where the users are both audience and actors, with the garden providing the changing scenery. Its inward-looking views invite participation. A clearly shaped opening into the space can be equated with a proscenium arch, and a colonnade the gallery – providing a notional separation between observer and observed. People look onto a space of fixed dimensions, but in this case, without the need for the suspension of disbelief.

The wall has been discussed as a barrier that restricts the view, preventing visual continuity to the horizon. The wall can be seen as a *picture plane*, distancing the observer from the external world. Openings allow us a glimpse of what might lie beyond the wall, framing what we see in a horizontal direction. If there are no openings, the upward view increases in significance, as we have seen in the traditional Islamic house, and the effect of the light coming directly downward also plays an important role in the design. These effects have been the subject of investigation in the twentieth century by artists such as James Turrell in many of his Skyspace projects.[8] He has created outdoor rooms with very large openings in their ceilings. *Figure 5.9.* Turrell is interested in the depth of space and how we

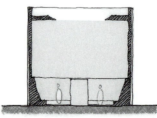

5.9
Section through Turrell's Skyspace room.

perceive it in relation to the external light quality. He is interested in the junction of ceiling and sky, where the space of the sky meets the space of the interior. For example, at twilight, the view up into the sky appears to be an opaquely painted surface, with no depth. Enclosed gardens, particularly if they are deep, are similarly affected.

The inward-looking enclosed garden can be a scene for observing the juxtaposition of natural and artificial components. The natural curves of trees and bushes of a well-planted garden can be offset by the sharper and more regular geometries of the architecture.

Within a small space, the details become very important. Pattern is used within smaller scale architectural components, such as the decorative tiles used particularly in countries around the Mediterranean. Tiles are used equally as components of building and garden. As they are small units, each can be seen in itself, or they can be used as component parts of a larger pattern, such as we see in many Islamic designs. *Figures 5.10, 5.11*.

5.10
Patterned tiles above a sink in the Viana garden.

5.11
Tiles around an entrance in the Alhambra.

Sensory seclusion

Four gardens

Each of the following case studies has been chosen for the way they invite our sensual engagement with the garden, and how this is achieved through integrating garden and architectural design.

Ritual and the everyday

An enclosed community

The first example is a design that relies just on one garden which is central to the surrounding buildings, and where *site* has been of critical importance. The Benedictine Monasterio de Las Condes[9] *Figure 5.13*, built in the 1960s, lies just below the crest of a hill above Santiago, Chile. The siting of the cloister garden in relation to its surroundings is significant. The building surrounds the garden on three sides, thus providing shelter in this exposed location, and the fourth side is opened up to the view. It looks over a valley filled with smog that hovers over the city, and across to the Andes. The garden refers to the magnitude of nature, and incidentally provides the space for us to reflect on how we have treated it. *Figure 5.14,*

The complex maintains the essential qualities of medieval monasteries, as well as being modernist in its conception and design. The enclosing walls read as solid planes punctuated with large areas of glass, framed in steel. *Figure 5.15*. The garden has been levelled from a steep north/south

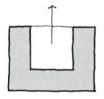

5.12
Central garden looking out.

5.13
Las Condes Monastery, Santiago, Chile.

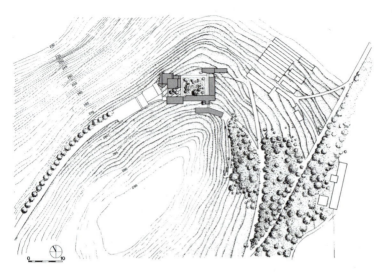

5.15
Las Condes cloister,
looking through to the
garden from the enclosed
cloister.

slope of the site and is laid out in a basic quadripartite plan, with a pool at the cross-over of the dividing paths. *Figure 5.16*. The edge condition has been considered separately, and particular attention has been given to the north and south sides. There is an open cloister to the south, more like a room than an external corridor. It provides enough shaded space for the monks to carry out a range of activities and be able to enjoy the view of the garden. A vine is trained across the openings in the cloister wall to provide additional shade in summer. *Figure 5.17*. The boundary to the north is no more than a low wall, the capping to a retaining wall beneath it. A wide path helps define the edge. A sense of enclosure has been achieved by the planting. Regularly placed potted plants line the path, and cypress trees have been planted on the hillside immediately below. Their natural thin columnar shapes frame and regulate the view to the gentle slopes of the farmed land and across to the snow-capped mountains.

5.16
Las Condes cloister garden, looking toward the pool.

5.17
Las Condes cloister garden. A vine grows against the columns, whose leaves provide shade from the sun during hot summer months, and allows light into the space throughout the winter when the leaves have fallen.

5.18
A fig tree in the middle
of the garden has been
trained to make a
shady canopy.

The planting within the cloister is abundant. Even in winter it is exuberant and colourful. The warm colours of the paving, where a mixture of materials has been used, predominantly brick ceramic tiles, with stone and concrete, are offset by the white walls of the building. Rills with simple sluices are positioned to regulate the water. A fig tree has been trained to form a canopy to provide shade for those who wish to sit in the garden in the long summer months. It attracts the birds, which is a good thing, but they eat all the figs, which is a little sad for the monks. *Figure 5.18.*

No restraint in planting has been shown, which is perhaps due to its particular inheritance of the original Spanish Catholics, with their Moorish influence, adapting to their new location with the rich soil and climate of the subtropics of South America. Unlike some of their counterparts in North Western Europe, the monks enjoy a close relationship with the land at many levels, through their agricultural work and their pleasure and enjoyment of a garden, so clearly evidenced by its well-tended beauty.

Ritual and event

Transformation of the everyday

The second garden also comprises a single central space, where the conversion of the surrounding buildings has been considered alongside the design of the garden. The old farmyard at Bury Court, Surrey, UK, has been transformed into a spectacular garden through the designs of Piet Oudolf.[10] *Figure 5.19.* It is set deep in the rolling countryside of the south

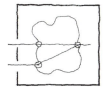

of England, and must be one of the most photographed places in Britain, through its capacity to hold events that make deep impressions on people's lives. For much of the year it is hired out for weddings and special occasions, to be endlessly revisited in photo albums. The buildings house all the necessary functions, but the garden, with some adaptations from the original design, sets the scene for making a public occasion into a memorable event. The house, barn and outbuildings that surround the garden have accumulated over many generations, but have never been conceived as a planned assemblage. The barn, housing the main function area, constitutes one of the sides. This is adjacent to a collection of outbuildings that have been converted into the business wing that make up the second side. The third comprises the family house, and the fourth side is defined by an old free-standing wall.

The layout has similarities to the monastic plan. The garden is the focus of all the buildings and opens directly from the reception area, and access between buildings is via a long corridor, equivalent to the covered cloister. Unlike a monastery though, the space has no higher spiritual purpose and is completely given over to being inhabited and enjoyed. There are spaces to accommodate large groups of people in some areas, and the intertwined paths around the perimeter provide a diversion for those who wish to go for a stroll or get away from the milling crowds. The scale of the plants and buildings bridges both public and private, so that when there are no events, it becomes the rear garden to the house. *Figure 5.21*. The garden accommodates and links the buildings in various ways through the positioning of its constituent parts such as flowerbeds, water, pavilion. The use of vistas and paths as ordering lines create visual links that provide an underlying structure to the design. *Figures 5.22, 5.23*. Balance takes precedence over symmetry in the overall composition, which works at many levels: shape,

5.21
Bury Court view from
veranda, which separates
the house from directly
opening onto the garden.

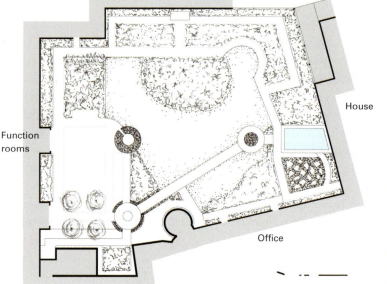

5.22
Bury Court site layout.

House

Function
rooms

Office

5.23
Schematic plan, ordering
lines shown in red.

texture, colour, seasonal variation. There are three complementary free-standing sculptural elements within the garden that give it an underlying geometry and tie it back to the building. Each provides a different focus as one walks around. Their overall plans have similar dimensions to that of the oast house, the most striking feature of the architectural backdrop (seen in outline on the plan) and may well be a reference to the design of the garden at Sissinghurst Castle.[11] One of these is a small steel-framed pavilion-like structure, fleshed out to give it density with a fine silvery texture by *pyrus salicifolia*. It invites you in and from there you can orient yourself for a journey into the garden and have a choice of several paths to follow. The major route leads directly toward a perfectly trimmed low box bush. *Figure 5.24.*

5.24
Looking toward the box bush.

The bush is not only a marker and focus, but acts as a pivot to swing you round to another path on a different axis that leads to the pond beside the house, or across the lawn to the third marker outside the barn.

In many places, plants have been placed directly against the buildings, giving a textural richness to the architecture, much of which is made of a warm red brick, local to this part of the country. The planting in the flowerbeds overlaps the paths, softening their edges. Wherever you go, a rich composition of colour, texture and form gives the qualities of a three-dimensional painting. The main flowerbed rustles and sways as a whole in the breeze. *Figure 5.25*. There is a small gap between the wall and the house. Like Mottisfont, it provides a discrete view of the outside world, a serene and pastoral countryside for the wedding guests, that cosily bolsters our ephemeral brush with Paradise.

5.25
Looking across one of the main flowerbeds.

Rooms in the town

Following a pattern of place making

The third example invites a discussion about gardens and architecture that connect through a weave of buildings and open spaces. It demonstrates how a design can evolve and expand over time using the same underlying principles of repeating the courtyard garden but in a very different way to the regularity of Pavia.

5.26
Patchwork of open spaces.

The Palacio de Viana sits in what is now the quiet suburb of Ajequía, Cordoba, Spain. It can be seen as a microcosm of the town. It originated in the fourteenth century, was privately owned until the twentieth century, and is now a museum. The continuing expansion of its patios was a way of not only creating favourable ambient climatic conditions in an area that has long hot summers, but also of providing living spaces outside the building envelope that are arguably as important as the internal ones adjacent to them. Each outdoor space has its own character, varying from public to private, formal to informal.

In the corner of a small square, bustling with people and traffic, there is a diagonally placed entrance portico that leads into a corner of a grand courtyard. *Figure 5.27*. This, including the colonnaded sides, is similar in dimensions to the square itself, but here the sounds of the city fade, and are replaced by the trickling fountain in the main courtyard, overlaid with birdsong. *Figure 5.28*. The bright light experienced outside the building is now muted and filtered by the tall palm tree that dominates the centre of the space. There are no direct spatial indicators of a route. A door at the end of one of the colonnades is the only visual cue to finding the next space, internal or external. The footprint of the Palace reveals that there are as many open outdoor spaces as there are internal ones. *Figures 5.29, 5.30*.

5.27
Viana Palace, Cordoba.
Entrance from the square.

Sensory seclusion

5.28
The reception courtyard.

5.29
Viana Palace ground floor
plan.

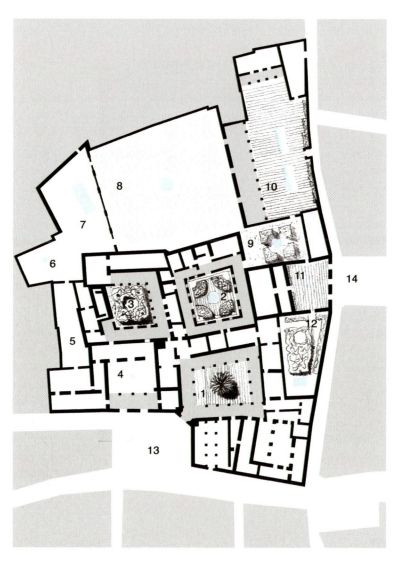

Key: Viana Palace

 1 Reception patio
 2 Archive patio
 3 Chapel patio
 4 Gate patio
 5 Gardener's patio
 6 Well patio
 7 Pool patio
 8 The garden
 9 Madame patio
10 Column patio
11 Grille patio
12 Orange tree patio
13 Plaza de Don Gome
14 Calle de las Rejas de Don
   Gome

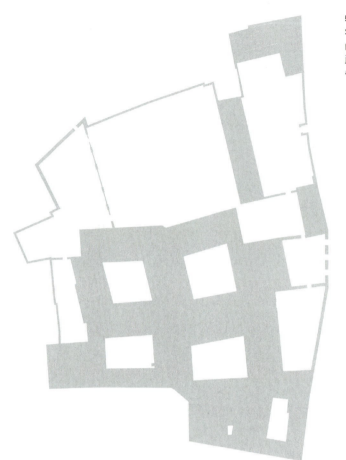

5.30
Simplified plan indicating
proportion and
juxtapositions of internal
and external spaces.

The patios and gardens work with the geometry of the building by absorbing its contrasting grids and irregular site boundaries. All the spaces feel very inhabitable. They each have different, but complementary, qualities, and vary in scale and proportion. There are those that are completely enclosed by buildings and walls and those that lead directly through to other spaces, those that have directed routes and those where you are left to wander freely, those that are purely functional and those that are purely pleasurable.

A pallet of components has been used – wells, fountains, seats, box hedging, trees, paving – that combine to give a rich variety of colourful planting. There is attention to detail, even in the most modest of spaces, such as the gardeners' courtyard. *Figures 5.31, 5.32.* Despite its interior nature, the Palace looks out to the city. The Grille courtyard visually connects through to the Calle de las Rejas de Don Gome, creating a formal set piece looking onto a little square, and the Gate Patio looks onto the Plaza de Don Gome, through a colonnaded wall which similarly brings together the villa and the city. *Figure 5.33.*

5.31
The garden, to explore and walk through at ground level, and to enjoy the pattern of it from the upper levels.

5.32
Viana Palace small courtyard.

5.33
The Grille courtyard, permanently on view from the steet, and overflowing with citrus trees planted against the wall and potted plants.

A very dense design has been refined over time through a consistent method of place making. The architectural ideas of each period have been absorbed, and do not distract from the unity of the whole. The scale is never overbearing. It embodies aspects of Romano/Islamic planning seen in smaller houses in Cordoba, together with the spatial connections of the urban fabric and formal garden layouts of the Renaissance. More open and orthogonal twentieth-century spaces have been added but unfortunately they lack the atmosphere of the older ones, despite the continuity with the other gardens. Pastiche has been relied on rather than trusting a modernist sensibility.

Rooms in the country

Challenging a way of living

By the beginning of the twentieth century much domestic architecture in England had become stifled by rules and codes of behaviour demanding that each room should have a particular function. It indicated a way of life bound by the empty formality and routine of the established patriarchal family. Even modestly sized houses had a proliferation of rooms that were organised by gender, class and function.[12] The conversion of Sissinghurst Castle and its grounds was conceived to challenge these rigid ideas. It was bought by Vita Sackville-West and her husband Harold Nicolson in 1930 when it was no more than a series of ruined buildings. It became a project that gradually brought the site to life over the next five years, and is now one of the most influential gardens of the twentieth century. Sissinghurst makes us examine domestic private space. It questions how we use rooms, and how they can be reinvented as the setting for experimentation and self-expression, challenging conventions of class, social hierarchy, monogamy and heterosexuality.[13]

The entire plot at Sissinghurst was conceived as a series of rooms, with designated activities. Vita had her writing room in the tower, the sitting room and library were combined within the Big Room in the North Wing. Breakfast would take place in the South Cottage where Harold had his work room and where he and Vita had their bedrooms. Eating took place outdoors whenever possible. Dinner would be amid the scent of the roses in the White Garden at the end of the day and through the dusk when the white flowers were at their best, their whiteness standing out against the fading light.[14] The pattern of the day necessitated walking outside to get from one activity to another through an orderly layout of outdoor rooms, each with their own distinct character.[15] It was achieved through both the structuring of the spaces and the planting, to elicit moods through colour, texture, scent, seasonal variation all appealing directly to the emotions. This was a radical step in garden design. Although it was a private garden, the Nicolsons opened it to the public in the late 1930s, a garden art gallery, and it has been visited ever since.

The footprint of the old sixteenth-century Tudor manor house has been used for locations for walls and hedges that now make up the site and divide it into separate areas. A disproportionately tall tower, all that is left of the manor house, which now stands apart from any other buildings, dominates the entire site. The long ascent of the tower is rewarded by a view of the entire garden, clearly showing its sculptural shaping. *Figure 5.35.* Not only is it a landmark, its central archway is the threshold to most of the garden. Once through, if you walk halfway across the Tower Lawn you are confronted with a choice. Small openings in the surrounding walls and hedges allow glimpses and arouse anticipation of three very contrasting journeys. *Figures 5.36, 5.37.*

The gap in the hedge directly ahead of you leads across to the informally planted orchard along a grassy path toward a statue of Dionysos (axis no. 1). If you turn to the left (axis no. 2), there is a framed view through an archway in a wall indicating an abundance of plants on the other side, enough to anticipate the much-celebrated White Garden. If you turn to the right, the view is similarly framed, but looks toward a much plainer area. If you follow this path, you come to the Rondel, drained of all colour apart from green, covered with only a lawn, and surrounded by a high circular wall of yew hedge.[16] The views out from here are restricted to four openings at right angles to each other. The axial route continues to the start of the Lime Walk in the Spring Garden. A statue acts as a pivot that rotates the axis of the path to be in line with the edge of the plot and the foundations of the original buildings (axis no. 3). The walk continues down to the side

5.34
Route and focus.

5.35
Sissinghurst, UK.
View from the tower.

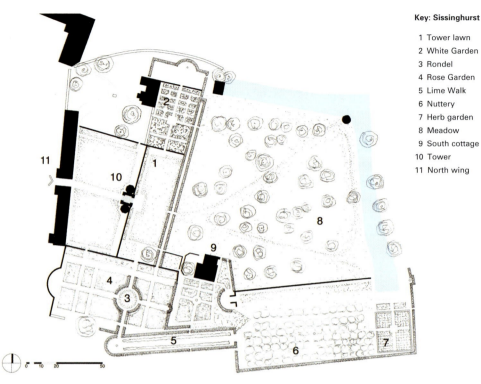

5.36
Sissinghurst site layout.

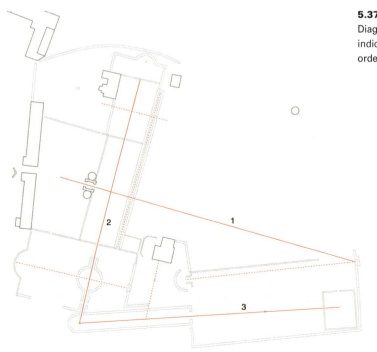

5.37
Diagrammatic analysis
indicating main axes and
ordering lines.

of the Nuttery, in line with the old moat wall, to the herb garden. Its centrally placed urn completes the long axis, and provides a destination in a similar manner to the central arbour of the White Garden that lies on the north boundary. *Figures 5.38–5.41.*

Although I have described these walks as being along strict axial alignments, the reality of the journey could not be more varied. The gardens are discrete and self-contained, rooms with their own character, with the equivalent to wall finishes, furniture and floor covering. You walk around the lawns, or along a path where the grid has been subdivided into smaller areas within the whole, variations of the themes of the Paradise garden with a fountain or urn in the middle and four paths leading away from it.

5.38
Sissinghurst. The Rondel.

5.39
Sissinghurst. Looking through a hole in the wall toward the Tower Lawn.

Such is the yew-walled White Garden, with its limited palette of green and white, and beds within orderly box hedges but overflowing with an abundance of shape, texture and scent that changes throughout the year. The arbour, covered with rosa mulliganii, makes a pavilion that unites the two parts of the garden. The Rondel, inside the Rose Garden, is as austere as the Rose Garden is full of colour and fragrance. Its proportions are closer to that of a building than a conventional garden space. You are invited to walk around it, instead of just walking straight through, to change your pace

5.40
Sissinghurst Lime Walk.

5.41
Sissinghurst White Garden.

Sensory seclusion

and enjoy its circularity. With its restricted views it hides the roses almost completely. There is just a hint of them from each opening, and the suggestion that comes airborne in the breeze.

The Lime Walk is regular and rhythmical; the well-behaved pleached trees form columns that structure this long corridor, and the hedges behind them form confining walls. As you walk down through the middle, the pattern of the shadows of the tree trunks evokes the shadows of a colonnade.

Sissinghurst is made memorable by a constant challenge to our senses, either by extremes of sensation or by denial. There are areas where colour dominates, or where the area is laden with scent, while in other areas colour is reduced down, and purity of form dominates. There is always a play between hard edges of wall and hedge and the sensuous shapes of the plants where they are left to grow into their natural forms.

These gardens demonstrate how designs that focus on sensory stimulation, achieved through a combination of enclosing architecture and well-chosen planting can become memorable places and enrich the quality of our lives. Sound, texture and smell and movement are as important as sight in the enclosed garden.

6 Detachment

The separation of the garden from the building

The Villa Lante

It is late summer, and the Lazio countryside above Rome is dried out and bleached. The days are still hot and the air is heavy. We have had a disappointing search for a garden close by in Soriano that has become completely hidden under the rubble of an ongoing restoration project. We come back to the small town of Bagnaia where we are staying for a few days, and walk into the town. The square is lively and not at all overrun by tourists, which is surprising because it is attached, quite literally, to one of the most astonishingly beautiful gardens of the Renaissance, the Villa Lante.[1]

Three splayed streets lead up the hill from the square, and two of them have very fine entrances at the end of them, promising garden and woodland beyond. *Figure 6.1*. We choose the central street and climb up to the grandest gate that we discover as we get closer is situated in another much smaller square, full of parked cars and an essential part of the tortuous through-traffic system. The gate is closed and we are directed to the other gate to our right, and enter the garden. We are taken to another world, just through the thickness of a wall, into the gardens of the Villa Lante.[2] The harsh sounds reflecting off the cobbled streets have gone. We can only hear the wind in the trees, the sound of running water, and our footsteps as we walk over the gravel path toward the formal gardens. The dry dusty browns and greys of the town have been replaced with shades of green of the trees and bushes all around us.

The first part of the garden we encounter is a very large and complex parterre, a virtuoso design, based around a central circular fountain within

6.1
Bagnaia, Italy. Looking up
to the entrance of the Villa
Lante from the square.

a square pool which is divided into four sections. The pools are surrounded by an intricate pattern of flowerbeds, framed with low box hedges.[3] As we walk in and around the parterre we see how it is lined up symmetrically with the main gate looking back to the town. If the gates were open, the parterre would visually connect through the little square and back down even further to the main square.

We look up and see it is also the end point of a complex of waterfalls that stretch down from as far as the eye can see. A continuous axis from the top of the hill is defined by this continuous flow of rushing water, that finally slows down and settles in the still pool of the parterre. *Figures 6.2, 6.3.* Our walk up the hill becomes a series of watery encounters, an elaborate dance around fountains, pools and cascades where the most

6.2
Villa Lante. Looking onto the parterre and beyond it to the town.

6.3
Villa Lante. Water
cascades down the hill,
with paths either side.

inventive and amazing water games are played. Whenever we arrive at one of these events, we can't necessarily see where to go, but the sound of distant water beckons us on, up steps and along terraces. The journey is enriched by dappled sunlight that penetrates through mature trees high over our heads and falls on the ground and the shimmering water. The stone steps and balustrades provide hot and cold corners, depending on the sun's position, and comfortable ledges to rest against. We climb to the top, eager to get to the end of our ascent and find the water source, the Grotto of the Deluge. It is sandwiched between two small and apparently identical casini.[4] *Figure 6.4.* The area to our left is raised up at least a metre from ground level, and not apparently accessible. *Figure 6.5*. On closer inspection we see that the casino adjacent to the higher level is a different shape to the other one and is considerably longer. We also discover that it has a hidden room, with a window looking onto the garden. At the far end there is an alcove housing a table, ready for feasting in complete seclusion. We notice one other opening, through the back wall and into the woods beyond. This tucked-away area has been called the Duchess's garden. Could this be a place for secret assignations, for those not wanting to announce their arrival, and where a hasty getaway could be arranged unnoticed?

This small, now somewhat neglected garden, the *giardino segreto*, is separated from the programme of the main garden. *Figure 6.6*. Although it

6.4
Villa Lante. The casino has two openings inside the little portico that look onto the raised garden. It has window seats, but no direct access.

6.5
Villa Lante. Alcove to the garden at the back of the casino.

6.6
Overview of the Villa
Lante, showing the
giardino segreto to one
side at the top.

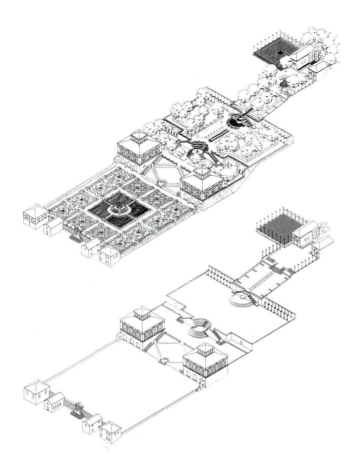

still conforms to an orthogonal plan, it breaks the rules of bi-symmetry that have been set up for the rest of the garden. Walls on two sides, and open colonnades on the other two, provide it with a sense of enclosure. There is a central pool and fountain, unfortunately now dry, and paths between four box-edged beds containing some neglected rose bushes. This simple garden is a counterpoint to the elaborate parterre on the lower terrace, as it has been stripped down to its essential form, maintaining the simplicity of the Islamic Chahar Bagh.

Detached gardens

The boundaries to enclosed gardens are not necessarily defined by the external walls of a building. This chapter will consider free-standing enclosed gardens, where they stand out as a statement in the landscape, or, paradoxically, are completely hidden. Their separateness often requires us to take a journey to get there, and this experience will have an affect on how we perceive them. The detached garden fulfils a range of needs and desires, and can broadly be split into two categories: gardens that can give access for our feelings – for matters of the heart, for privacy, thought and reflection – and those for the specialised production of plants, such as the botanic garden and the kitchen garden.

Giardino segreto

By the late Renaissance, design strategies for gardens were devised to incorporate urban life and link it back to the natural world. The experience of the Renaissance garden could also be appreciated as a theatrical event. Narratives were superimposed onto a landscape that would unfold and express contemporary philosophical ideas through the layout and iconography, which would be revealed as you walked from one space to another. Many gardens were developed as a series of linked outdoor rooms, such as the terraces at the Villa Lante, or the gardens of the Villa Farnese. Both refer back to antiquity, and applied new theories of beauty based on mathematical proportion, perspective and harmony.

Axes, imagined straight lines, were set up as ways of linking a series of these rooms and were the means of connecting across large tracts of land. Water often played an important role in indicating this connection. Axes were treated as continuous linear elements of the design rather than the centri-focal locations of the fountains of the closed Islamic garden. The architects and hydraulic engineers of that period excelled themselves with inventive displays.[5]

With the larger grander programme, also came a desire for more separate hidden, quiet spaces that did not need to strictly conform to the geometrical rules. The *giardino segreto*, the hidden garden, evolved where the formal rules could be broken, and an element of surprise could be introduced.

The hidden garden

And then she took a long breath and looked behind her up the long walk to see if any one was coming. No one was coming. No one ever did come, it seemed, and she took another long breath, because she could not help it, and she held back the swinging curtain of ivy and pushed the door which opened slowly – slowly.

Then she slipped through it, and shut it behind her, and stood with her back against it, looking about her, and breathing quite fast with excitement, and wonder, and delight.

She was standing inside the secret garden.[6]

Frances Hodgson Burnett immortalised the secret garden in her novel of the same name at the beginning of the twentieth century, and it has captured children's imaginations ever since. The idea of the secret garden lives in our adult imaginations as much as within the real landscape, as I have discovered for myself. For many years the botanic gardens of the university here where I live had been abandoned, overgrown and forgotten by all but a few. It was a pleasure to open the stiff iron gate, pass along a narrow path by the dilapidated greenhouses with remnants of experiments still in evidence, and wander into an accidentally created wilderness where nature was reasserting itself, cut off from the landscaping of the rest of the university. Stumbling across a hidden place arouses our curiosity and, as we have seen at the Villa Lante, the *giardino segreto* can be a very desirable place.

The hidden garden displays certain characteristics: First, it is out of our expected field of vision, whether we are in the city or the country, and away from the main routes and thoroughfares. It is essentially private. Second, it has to be 'discovered', indicating the necessity of the journey to get there, that might provoke an emotional response, of anticipation or even mystery.[7] There will be an indication of something to find and discover that may contradict the layout of the rest of the location. Third, it is a place where visitors can feel safe enough to access their emotions. These characteristics are frequently found in children's stories, the memories of which remain with us. Separateness gives it a particular quality of being special, and enclosure gives it a sense of interior that equates with our interior emotional landscapes. A separate space has always seemed fitting for personal memories, a place where we can concentrate and reflect on our lives, the human condition and the cosmos.

Escape refuge in the town

Gardens hidden in towns can be striking through the contrast to their urban context. There is the pleasure of discovery for a visitor. There is also the enjoyment of a detailed knowledge of the fine grain of a city, where hidden areas can be returned to and be absorbed into the patterns of daily life.

The Phoenix Garden in central London, for example, is hidden within the fabric of the city with a townscape of skyscrapers towering over it; it will only be discovered by the intrepid, who enjoy walking through the inner arteries of the city. The garden is a refuge created by the local community, but open to the public during the daytime in a place where open space, let alone planting, is hard to find. It provides an urban oasis, a venue for moments of private intimacy. *Figure 6.7.*

Publicly accessible outdoor spaces are rarely designed into new-build architectural schemes. An exception to this lies in the middle of the historic

town of Winchester, UK. The town has been inhabited since the Roman occupation and has old and new buildings juxtaposed throughout the town, creating many incidental spaces and alleyways. When part of the County Offices[8] was re-planned in the 1980s, the design had to accommodate a listed tree and a public right of way. The decision was made to take advantage of this rather than treat it as a hindrance. A garden, containing the tree, can now be seen through a wide opening in the building from the street. *Figure 6.8.* The view is framed by the opening, inviting pedestrians into a small enclosed garden. Once you are inside the garden it feels quite private. The surrounding tall buildings seem to protect you, and the view back to the street keeps you in touch with the city. At the back of the garden, the right of way continues as part of Winchester's footpaths that are woven into the fabric of the town.

The excitement of finding a hidden garden is often due to its un-expectedness. When I was photographing the Dean Garnier Garden behind Winchester Cathedral, I overheard a mother say to her young daughter 'Come and have a look at the secret garden.' The large heavy wooden door, greying with age and set within a windowless wall gives little away. On closer observation there are three very small openings carved out beside the latch giving the merest hint of what lies on the other side. It creaks open, and a stone retaining wall straight ahead blocks the view, but there is a small flight of steps to the right that invite you up. At the top, an upper-level garden is revealed, a raised enclosed terrace sitting on the site of the monks' dormitory. It is removed from the ground plane, and looks across to the cathedral. It is laid out somewhat literally to reflect the interior spaces of the cathedral. A rose covered pergola divides the nave and choir areas. The third section, the Lady Chapel garden, is hidden from sight, private and secluded, and can only be discovered when you have reached the far end of the garden. *Figures 6.9, 6.10, 6.11.*

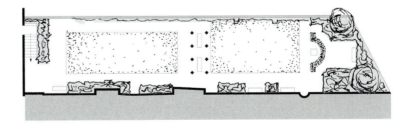

6.9
Dean Garnier Garden.
Plan.

6.10
Winchester, UK. Entrance
to Dean Garnier Garden,
with three small spy holes.

6.11
Dean Garnier Garden.
View across the garden.

Detachment

Reflection

Private memory

Enclosed gardens are often used to remember people and events. The garden provides a safe place and can be a setting for accessing difficult memories and emotions, allowing the visitor to experience and confront their fears and senses of loss. Such a place is the very quiet Little St Mary's churchyard, in the heart of Cambridge, UK. Church and churchyard take up a plot just off one of the main streets, adjacent to a narrow lane that leads toward the river.

As you approach the churchyard it appears to be overgrown, but as soon as you walk around, it becomes apparent that you are in a carefully tended wild garden. At one point you can see a narrow curving path that disappears round a corner of the church. *Figure 6.12*. The light is inviting

6.12
Little St Mary's, Cambridge, UK. Path leading to the hidden garden.

and intriguing, although it seems to be leading to an even more overgrown and forgotten corner. The path leads to a very small space, enclosed by buildings rising high above it, and the atmosphere is very calm. You cross a camomile lawn, and its fragrance rises as you walk over it to a bench. There is a plaque above the bench, placed there in memory of a loved one who died young. The words, hand-carved into smooth grey slate, contribute to the mood. Most visitors will not know who this young woman was, but the memorial acts as a reminder of our own mortality. Through the selective planting and organising of a leftover space, instead of being neglected, it has become a very special place. It is also a garden of remembrance – there are many names set in the grass at one end of the garden.

Public memory

Enclosed gardens are often used to commemorate public events. There are many memorial gardens commemorating those who lost their lives in wartime. The Garden of Exile and Emigration at the Jewish Museum in Berlin, designed by Daniel Libeskind is a place for collective memory, and reflection.[9] Its message, and hence our experience, is very different to that of any pleasure garden. It attempts 'to completely disorientate the visitor. It represents a shipwreck of history'.[10] *Figure 6.13.* The journey starts at the end of a dramatic journey through the museum where many preconceptions of architecture have already been challenged. You emerge from the museum through an underground link into an open space unlike any other, and undergo a sensory experience of extremes, through disorientation and the unexpected. Instead of the reassurance of a garden surrounded by plants

6.13
Garden of Exile and Emigration, Jewish Museum, Berlin. Aerial view.

and flowerbeds, you are in a maze of tilted columns. They rise from a twice-tilted ground plane making it hard to balance on, as if you were at sea. *Figure 6.14.* This is exaggerated by the pebbled ground surface, which is set considerably below the natural ground level. It is so disorienting that people have been known to come out feeling nauseated. The columns comprise an orderly grid of seven rows of seven concrete shafts, seven metres high. They are at right angles to the floor plate, and so you don't read them as being tilted when you move around. Forty-eight of the columns are filled with earth from Berlin, and the central forty-ninth column is filled with earth from Jerusalem. The thickness of the columns in relation to the spaces between them limits the perception of spatial continuity, which increases your unease. Only by looking up do you see the vegetation. Despite being lower than ground level, you are below the trees, and even their roots. All the columns are planted with willow oak trees at the top of them that will withstand the Berlin microclimate. They represent olive trees, traditional Jewish symbols of peace and hope. *Figure 6.15.* The view from outside is

6.14
Garden of Exile and Emigration. Inside the garden.

6.15
Garden of Exile and
Emigration. Looking
toward the garden.

very different. The garden appears as a sculptural whole, set in the context of the museum and the city of Berlin, emerging from the lowered ground level. In summer the trees cap the garden to make a complete canopy, and together with the columns create a single regulated geometric form. The columns can be translated as the oversized tree trunks of a single stand of a plantation and provide a clear comprehensible shape within the city. Their closeness to each other makes the overall volume distinct. The garden, like the museum, is layered with metaphor, and creates an overwhelming atmosphere open to personal interpretations as much as a response to the more obvious symbolism. We cannot help but be moved by it.

Neutralising territory

Enclosed gardens can make a contribution to resolving a wide range of social problems, and in ways that are not necessarily apparent. In 2005, Office architects[11] won a competition for the design of a border control point between Mexico and the United States. The solution to the problem of defining the nature of this potentially tense zone was to create a garden. It was, both literally and metaphorically, an oasis in the desert. *Figures 6.16, 6.17.* The hope was to defuse tension instead of enforcing control. The garden, a gridded canopy of palm trees, stands out in contrast to prevailing desert conditions, a place to slow down and take stock. The rectilinear border garden has high adobe walls with one opening cut each side of the border. The control points and administrative offices comprise two cool

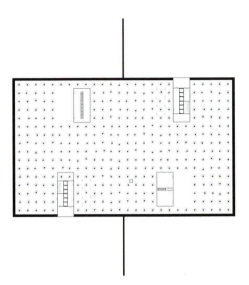

6.16
Plan for the border between Mexico and the USA.

6.17
Border between Mexico and the USA.
Image of the border as an oasis.

pavilions within the garden, nestling under a canopy of trees. It is a very non-aggressive solution to the problem of border conflicts and tensions. Although the scale and function is very different to the courtyard of the Mesquite in Cordoba, it has aspects in common. It provides a transitional space with a ceiling of trees, in this case the crowns of palm trees, to provide a cooler shaded area underneath, that takes you calmly from one place to the other, in preparation for entering a different country with different cultural values. The architects' direct pragmatic approach challenged 'architectural' solutions to the questions posed, defying any conventional architectural rhetoric. If it had been built, it could perhaps have eased the tension of border control in a passive way. Instead of the conventional utilitarian or even hostile outposts, there would be a garden, indicating unity rather than intolerance, calm instead of violence.

The productive garden

Science and horticulture

Botanic and kitchen gardens are designed with the specific aim of optimising growing conditions for plants. Location in relation to topography and climate take precedence over visual considerations. Botanic gardens developed in Europe during the sixteenth century concurrent with advances being made in the sciences. Walled kitchen gardens flourished from the seventeenth to the nineteenth centuries. Landowners demanded to be well fed, and there was also a taste for the exotic. In Britain, with the developing empire and the popularity of the Grand Tour, people would bring back plants as trophies from all over the world. Shiploads of plant species started to be relocated in new habitats. This necessitated making suitable environmental conditions to keep them alive.

The wall

The wall is the controlling element of the early botanic gardens, kitchen gardens and even the *giardini segreti*, where we may often find it substituted by a hedge. It is the wall that provides spatial definition and a sense of enclosure and will protect the interior from unwanted external conditions. It is the wall that has thermal mass, with the capacity to absorb heat during the day and radiate it out as the external temperature cools. It provides support for plants that can be trained to allow them maximum exposure to the sun. The wall also provides support for glass houses, and buildings for the gardeners, where plants can be stored and prepared, and where tools can be kept and maintained. Making an opening in it creates an entrance. The gap in the wall is a threshold that indicates at a symbolic level that we are about to enter or exit somewhere that is different. This one element, the wall, continues to be a defining element.

Outdoor room as laboratory – the botanic gardens

In Jane Smiley's novel *Duplicate Keys*, Henry, a botanist at the New York Botanic Garden, shows Alice the gardens for the first time:

> They stepped down from the formal promenade into, and among, the more spacious spreading of grass and lilac bushes covered with white lavender, and magenta blossoms. Alice gasped, both at the sight and the sweet fragrance. 'The Botanic Garden,' he went on, 'is actually a fairly thriving ecosystem.'
> 'It's like heaven.'
> 'Yes,' Henry said, 'it is . . .'[12]

Alice's response to the garden and this exchange between the two friends encapsulates how many of us feel about botanic gardens. Although there is no direct aesthetic agenda, the layout of plants by classification often gives much satisfaction to visitors. They stand out in urban surroundings as earthly paradises, as well as fulfilling their functions as places of scientific research, and educational resources. Since they were established, the layouts have undergone many changes. With shifts of scientific discovery, plants have constantly had to submit to new positions and have overflowed beyond the original garden boundaries as more species have been found and added to existing collections.

History and development

Botanic gardens were born out of a desire for a rational connection between nature and ourselves, through the observation of plants. They were open-air laboratories, created so that we might be able to comprehend the orders of the natural world through scientific enquiry. They were established for 'glorifying God's creation and studying what wonders he had wrought in the plant world'.[13] The walled enclosure with its own microclimate creates ideal environmental conditions for such investigation to take place. There is evidence of botanic gardens as early as the Moorish palaces of Seville and Toledo in Spain, where scientific plant collections were recorded in the eleventh and twelfth centuries.[14] The *hortus botanicus* emerged in the sixteenth century in several European cities, attached to universities such as Leiden, Padua, Pisa and Oxford. They evolved from the earlier physic or medicinal gardens.

As scientific advances of the Middle East influenced European botanists, it was considered appropriate to use the layout of the well-established Islamic garden as a model, where pure geometry underpinned the design. This concurred with the emphasis laid on the importance of regular geometries, phyllotaxis,[15] found in plants. There was also a connection with the cloister garden of the Christian church, *hortus conclusus*, and its reference to the Garden of Eden. By collecting plants from all corners of the earth, the natural world could be observed under controlled conditions with the hope of shedding light on the lost Eden. In botanic gardens the streams of the Islamic garden were transformed into footpaths providing access to the flowerbeds. They became living encyclopedias.[16] This arrangement, where the conflict between the demands of geometry and classification were resolved, has contributed to the uniqueness of the typology of these early botanic gardens. Organising plants by genus took priority over composition based on shape, form or colour. Some were very successful and had a commercial value as well as a scientific one, particularly when horticulture became more fashionable. Research has been continuous, although much of it now takes place in the laboratory. The modern global need for food and renewable resources coupled with climate change has necessitated more experimentation and this need has put botanical gardens back at the forefront, with new establishments being set up such as the extension to Kew Botanic Gardens at Wakehurst Place, UK.[17] As well as housing one of the largest seed banks in the world, it has laboratories and educational outdoor classrooms laid out with a view to the future, to the possibilities of growing crops with higher yields and for developing materials that can be used in the building industry, cosmetics and medicine. The early gardens, however, are also in need of re-evaluation, to understand their economic use of space, the importance of aspect and their use of low-energy technological methods used for propagation and yield.

Padua

The Orto Botanico at Padua, established in 1545, has survived intact. It was placed in a sheltered area of Padua, close to existing streams that would guarantee a continuous water supply. *Figure 6.18.* The enclosing wall is circular, which in turn encloses a perfect square layout of planting beds. The square is divided up into a quadripartite plan with paths between the

6.18
Padua Botanic Garden. Engraving of the original layout.

beds. There are four entrances, one at each cardinal point. *Figures 6.19, 6.20.* It also followed patterns of the parterres fashionable at the time, though the detailed arrangement was based on accommodating the ordering and classification systems of the plants. Girolamo Porro, an artist who was commissioned to draw a plan of the plant beds and publish a guide to the gardens for students of botany in the form of a notebook (*L'orto*

6.19
Padua Botanic Garden. Engraving showing the garden in winter.

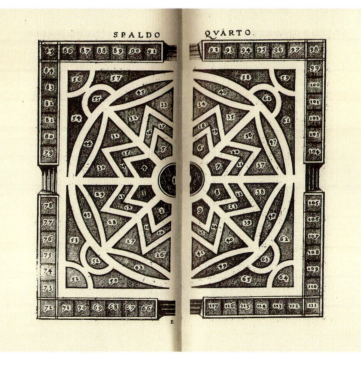

6.20
Padua Botanic Garden. Pages from a notebook for students, *L'orto de i semplici di Padova*, 1591, indicating layout of the beds.

de i semplici di Padova, 1591), talks of the desire to contain 'the world in a chamber'. The garden's status was reflected in the design of its enclosure. There is a substantial enclosing brick wall, over four metres high, capped elegantly with stone, with imposing entrances. Although the city has now encroached on all sides, it would originally have stood out on its own, rivalled only by the churches nearby.

Oxford

Botanic gardens are some of the few places where the demands of science and education are shared with desire to escape and to be close to nature. The University of Oxford Botanic Garden lies on the outskirts of the town and is as well known for being a place to escape from the bustle of the streets, packed with students, tourists and traffic, as it is for its research. The garden has many benches, wide walkways and lawns to walk and sit on. Like Padua it was one of the first botanic gardens to be established in Europe.[18] The design of the original area was a pure square divided into the quadripartite plan, with a central fountain, but with a series of rectilinear planting beds. *Figures 6.21, 6.22*. Larger than Padua, it has been able to adapt its contents within its boundaries over several hundred years. The beds have undergone a new change of layout as the classification of plant families is now based on evolutionary relationships discovered through the use of molecular biology. The resultant display underpinned by contemporary scientific theory brings with it a new shape to the composition

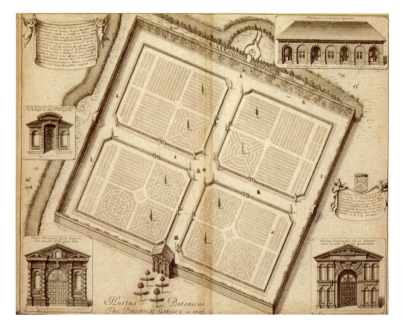

6.21
Oxford Botanic Garden. Engraving of original layout.

of the beds. The stone gateway at the entrance is even grander than that of Padua,[19] indicative of its original stature. It is more of an elaborate sculpture than a gateway. It gives the garden a public face that in the seventeenth century overtly celebrated its importance. As our attitudes have changed and the botanic garden is open to the public every day, we now slip though a small opening in the wall beside the old entrance, and go through a new ticket office more appropriate for the twenty-first century. *Figure 6.23.* The walls are always present in the background, protecting us, so we can roam freely in a garden that celebrates science rather than the importance or wealth of an individual.

6.23
Oxford Botanic Garden.
View of entrances, old
and new.

Nourishment – the kitchen garden

> The kitchen garden was to be next admired, and he led the way to it across a small portion of the park.
>
> The number of acres contained in this garden was such as Catherine could not listen to without dismay, being more than double the extent of all Mr Allen's, as well her father's, including the churchyard and orchard. The walls seemed countless in number, endless in length; a village of hothouses seemed to arise among them, and a whole parish to be at work within the enclosure. The general was flattered by her looks of surprise, which told him almost as plainly, as he soon forced her to tell him in words, that she had never seen any garden at all equal to them before; . . . '. . . He loved a garden. Though careless enough in most matters of eating, he loved good fruit – or if he did not, his friends and children did. There were great vexations, however, attending such a garden as his. The utmost care could not always secure the most valuable fruits. The pinery[20] had yielded only one hundred in the last year. Mr Allen, he supposed, must feel these inconveniences as well as himself.'
>
> Jane Austen, *Northanger Abbey*,
> first published 1818

Kitchen gardens are close relatives to botanic gardens, but they date back much further, to the very first walled enclosures of the Middle East, the *Pairidaeza* of ancient Persia. Botanic gardens are few, but kitchen gardens, based on the same principle of the enclosing wall, are plentiful. In Britain they flourished in the eighteenth and nineteenth centuries, when it was fashionable for wealthy landowners to grow exotic plants as well as providing food for the large number of people who worked on the estate. These estates were, in effect, self-sufficient. Some of the more innovative gardens could produce fruit and vegetables such as melons on 'hot beds', fermenting boxes of manure and straw. Heated walls were invented for frost protection in winter.

Until the end of the seventeenth century kitchen gardens in Britain were close to the house and integrated with the overall garden design. By the end of the eighteenth century, with the advent of the English Landscape Garden and the Picturesque, formal planning was abandoned and a rectilinear walled garden was thought to be discordant with the 'naturalistic' views of the estate. The kitchen garden was removed, and positioned so that it was out of sight. This banishment had several advantages. It could be chosen for its aspect, fertility, or closeness to water. Walls grew in height, and intricate and inventive uses of glass abounded.

The beds were laid out in an orderly manner, often maintaining an overall quadripartite plan, and their width was determined by the length of a gardener's reach. The sheltered interior of the kitchen garden speeded up production and prolonged the growing season. *Figure 6.24*. Aspect was important. Any planting against a south-facing wall had an increased yield. The art of espaliered trees developed, training fruit trees two-dimensionally against a wall, so that all the fruit could receive as much sunlight as possible. *Figure 6.25*. Many walls were glazed, and turned into glasshouses. These could be heated in winter and extend the range of possibilities for rare foods and flowers for the dining room table.

6.24
Trengwainton kitchen garden (1814), Cornwall, UK. Beds in the kitchen garden are tilted toward the angle of the sun to maximize solar gain.

6.25
Espaliered plum and pear trees. Branches are only one layer thick, so that all fruit can benefit from full sunlight.

The garden's removal from the main vistas necessitated a walk to get there, and the journey itself was an experience of anticipation. Nothing would be revealed until you had entered the garden through a modest gate set in the wall. As kitchen gardens were conceived as functional spaces, the entrance was not celebrated as it was in botanic gardens. By the nineteenth century it became fashionable for kitchen gardens to become decorative as well as useful. Such gardens are often referred to as *potagers*,[21] combining horticultural expertise and virtuosity. *Figure 6.26*. They were poetic in spirit, and in some cases even referred back to classical Roman texts.[22]

6.26
Val Joanis potager, France. Equal emphasis made on display and production.

6.27
Val Joanis potager. Covered walkway.

Inside the garden, walkways were often planted with colonnades trained with vines or pleached fruit trees to provide shade. *Figure 6.27*. There might be benches and small gazebos[23] to sit in, or a fountain in the middle. The fountain still provided a pleasing effect, even though by now it had lost its religious symbolism. Vegetables were juxtaposed with flowers, taking into account their colour, shape and form.

These gardens were very labour intensive and relied on low wages. After the First World War when there were not enough men to tend the gardens and the cost of labour rose, they could not be maintained and were all but lost. Since the latter part of the twentieth century, with increased public and corporate ownership, some of the great kitchen gardens have been revived, and have again become popular places to visit. Like botanic gardens, they have a new life through their use in horticultural experimentation as well as a widely held belief in the therapeutic aspect of gardening.

Revival and reinvention

The kitchen garden at Audley End, UK,[24] has undergone a major transformation, from dense wild undergrowth to a working garden. Its location is set back from the main house and completely hidden from view by a clump of carefully planted trees. *Figure 6.28*. Its sharp edges contrast with the soft eighteenth-century landscaping in which the house sits. After years of neglect it is now being revived and reinvented. It is very much a working garden with no place for sentiment. *Figure 6.29*. There are contraptions to keep the birds out rather than bring them in. The raucous

6.28
Audley End, UK. Aerial view showing the kitchen garden out of sight from the house.

6.29
Audley End. The kitchen
garden has been turned
into an efficient working
garden again.

sound of crows is transmitted electronically, rather than any attempt to encourage the sweet song of the thrush. It has a roughness that is a relief from the immaculate trimming and tidying of pleasure gardens. Its charm to the visitor comes out of utility based on an understanding of the local conditions of land and climate.

The main kitchen garden is a large enclosure, surrounded by a wall that is rarely lower than 2.4m high. It is trapezoidal rather than rectilinear, with the wider side at the south end. The original idea was to funnel warmed air down toward the south end, and maximise the heating of this part of the garden. The west wall was originally constructed to house a series of fires placed at intervals along its length that would circulate warm smoke along internal air passages, and prevent new growth on the espalier trees being frosted. The glasshouses are still full of exotic plants, such as grapes, figs, oranges, peaches and tomatoes, all of which need protection in the UK. *Figure 6.30*. They are positioned along the south-facing boundary wall, maximising solar gain through the glass. Heat is stored within the thermal mass of the brick wall. A ventilation scheme has been devised to prevent overheating, comprising large sliding sashes of panels of glass controlled very simply with a counterweight system. *Figure 6.31*. On the outer side of the same wall there is a series of buildings that house all the activities that need to be under cover, such as the potting and nurturing of delicate plants, storage, the boiler room, the head gardener's office. This is the human side, and although it is the garden headquarters, it is interesting to reflect that it was located on the other side of the wall, outside of paradise. Audley End as a kitchen garden in the twenty-first century goes beyond heritage and is being transformed into a viable working area, part of a growing movement that is encouraging local sustainable food production.[25] It is an inspiration for a *pairidaeza* for the twenty-first century.

6.30
Audley End. Vines kept
alive in the greenhouse.

6.31
Audley End.
Counterweights for large
sliding sashes.

All these gardens owe their existence to reasons that go beyond desire, pleasure and enjoyment, and fulfil a particular needed role within their own contexts. Many are hidden, and revealed through a process of discovery. The secret garden is often camouflaged in order not to attract attention. The botanic garden, in contrast, advertises itself and celebrates its status. Kitchen gardens have been firmly placed in the landscape, but in most cases, such as at Audley End, they were often disguised and took second place to the layout of the perfected naturalistic landscape of the main garden. Only now are they being reassessed and gaining a new status as our values shift.

Epilogue

Finding good examples of enclosed gardens from the twentieth and twenty-first centuries has been more of a struggle than looking further into the past. There is a wealth of good buildings and fine gardens, but recently the 'object' building has prevailed and, with some notable exceptions, the inclusion of an enclosed garden or even a courtyard garden within contemporary designs has not been favoured. But perhaps, with the increasing need to pay attention to changing climatic conditions, it is the time to re-evaluate the enclosed garden. We can no longer avoid rethinking our relationship with nature, and must respect it. We can start by celebrating the natural world as an integral part of our designs. Enclosed gardens – outdoor rooms – where site and orientation are taken into account, can be created with very low impact and economy of means. Enclosing a garden gives us opportunities not only for close observation, but also to reassess the precarious balance between the natural world and our own impositions on it. The annual pavilion design for the Serpentine Gallery in central London in 2011 is by architect Peter Zumthor, together with garden designer Piet Oudolf, and is based on the concept of the *hortus conclusus*. In Zumthor's words:

> The building acts as a stage, a backdrop for the interior garden of flowers and light. Through blackness and shadow one enters the building from the lawn and begins the transition into the central garden, a place abstracted from the world of noise and traffic and the smells of London – an interior space within which to sit, to walk, to observe the flowers. This experience will be intense and memorable, as will the materials themselves – full of memory and time.

Through looking at historical precedent, it is clear that enclosed gardens have been in use continuously in many parts of the world. It seems apparent that at some level we are hard-wired into the desire for paradise on earth, and that we want to represent it as a garden. Different generations and societies have had many ways of expressing this desire. Are we still seeking paradise in the twenty-first century?

Notes

1 Defining the territory: the ambiguous nature of an enclosed garden

1 Mottisfont Abbey was originally an Augustinian thirteenth-century priory, and lived in as a private house until the mid-twentieth century, and now owned by the National Trust.

2 Rob Aben and Saskia de Wit, *The Enclosed Garden,* 1999, Rotterdam: 010 Publishers.

3 Hidcote Manor, Gloucestershire, UK, created by Lawrence Johnston; started in 1907.

4 Vittorio Gregotti, 'Editoriale', *Rassegna*, 1 Dec. 1979.

5 Dorothy Graham, *Chinese Gardens*, 1973, New York: Dodd, Mead & Company.

6 The region of North Africa that includes Morocco, Algeria, Tunisia, Libya, Mauritania and Western Sahara.

7 Hassan Fathy, *Natural Energy and Vernacular Architecture. Principles and Examples with Reference to Hot Arid Climates*, 1986, Chicago: University of Chicago Press.

8 Ibid.

9 Brian Edwards *et al.*, *Courtyard Housing: Past, Present and Future*, 2005, London: Taylor & Francis.

10 The Mesquite has been adapted for Christian worship since the thirteenth century, but still maintains the essential structure of the mosque, with a continuous regular grid of columns.

11 D. Fairchild Ruggles, *Islamic Gardens and Landscapes*, 2008, Philadelphia: University of Pennsylvania Press.

12 It is thought that the garden was originally created for the benefit of the workers who looked after the mosque, as it is very unusual to have a planted garden associated with mosques.

13   D. Fairchild Ruggles, *Islamic Gardens and Landscapes*, p. 90.

14   There has been much debate over the validity and symbolic meaning of the trees, and their appropriateness for a mosque courtyard. See Fairchild Ruggles, *Islamic Gardens and Landscapes*.

15   A detailed analysis can be found in Aben and de Wit, *The Enclosed Garden*.

16   The New Gardens were planted in the 1930s.

17   Jill Billington, *London's Parks and Gardens*, 2003, Singapore: Tien Wah Press.

18   Designed by architects Patel Taylor and landscape architects Group Signes (Allain Provost).

19   The Thames Barrier is a moveable flood barrier, completed 1982.

20   Jill Billington, *London's Parks and Gardens*.

21   Niall Kirkwood, ed., *Manufactured Sites: Rethinking the Post-industrial Landscape*, 2001, London: Taylor & Francis.

2 From patio to park: the enclosed garden as a generator of architectural and landscape design

1   Markus Breitschmid, *The Significance of the Idea in the Architecture of Valerio Olgiati*, 2008, Zurich: Verlag Niggli AG, Sulgen.

2   Terraced housing is used widely in Britain as terminology for row housing.

3   Quoted from Gennaro Postiglione, ed., *One Hundred Houses for One Hundred European Architects of the Twentieth Century*, 2008, Cologne: Taschen.

4   Charles Jencks and Edwin Heathcote, *The Architecture of Hope. Maggie's Cancer Caring Centres*, 2010, London: Frances Lincoln.

5   Open spaces in Cambridge university colleges are traditionally described as courts, and in Oxford as quadrangles.

6   TER Landscape Architects, 1993.

7   Aben and de Wit, *The Enclosed Garden*.

8   Ibid.

9   Mark Girouard, *Cities and People*, 1985, New Haven, CT: Yale University Press, pp. 224–5.

10   John Summerson, *The Architecture of the Eighteenth Century*, 1969, London: Thames and Hudson, p. 163.

11   *Flaneur*, much celebrated by Baudelaire in nineteenth-century Paris, literally a *stroller* in the city, one who enjoys the experience of it for its own sake.

3 Taming nature – and the way to paradise

1   Elisabeth B. MacDougall and Richard Ettinghausen, eds, *The Islamic Garden*, 1976, Washington, DC: Dumbarton Oaks.

2   John Prest, *The Garden of Eden, the Botanic Garden and the Re-creation of Paradise*, 1981, New Haven, CT: Yale University Press, p. 18.

3   Anne Michaels, *The Winter Vault*, 2009, London: Bloomsbury.

4   Emma Clark, *The Art of the Islamic Garden*, 2004, Marlborough, Wilts: Crowood Press.

5   Elizabeth Moynihan, *Paradise as a Garden*, 1979, London: Scolar Press.

6 Ibid.

7 Vitruvius, first century BCE is best known for his *Ten Books on Architecture*, and for stating that good architecture should exhibit *firmitas, utilitas, venustas*, firmness, commodity and delight.

8 A.R. Littlewood, 'Ancient Literary Evidence for the Pleasure Gardens of Roman Country Villas', in Elisabeth B. MacDougall & Wilhelmina F. Jashemski, eds, *Ancient Roman Villa Gardens*, 1987, Washington, DC: Dumbarton Oaks.

9 Farrar, *Ancient Roman Gardens*.

10 *Hortus conclusus* comes from the Latin; literally translated as 'enclosed garden', and much used metaphorically, associated with the Virgin Mary in medieval and early Renaissance art and poetry.

11 The King James 1st Bible, Song of Solomon, 4: 12–16 (AV).

12 Anne Jennings, *Medieval Gardens*, 2004, London: English Heritage, pp. 51–2.

13 John Harvey, *Medieval Gardens*, 1990, London: B. T. Batsford.

14 Ibid. p. 60.

15 *Le Roman de la Rose* started off by Guillaume de Lorris, in the late 1230s, was completed 40 years later by Jean de Meun.

16 British Library online gallery: http://www.bl.uk/onlinegallery/onlineex/remark manu/roman/

17 *Hortus delicarium* – the garden of delights.

18 MacDougall and Ettinghausen, *The Islamic Garden*.

19 Prest, *The Garden of Eden*.

20 Chahar Bagh comes from the Persian: *châr*, meaning four, and *bâgh* meaning garden.

21 Fairchild Ruggles, *Islamic Gardens and Landscapes*.

22 Translated by Raymond P. Scheindlin, Masoret (1995) 5(1): 3. From Roald Hoffmann and Shira Leibowitz Schmidt, *Old Wines New Flasks: Reflections on Science and the Jewish Tradition*, New York: W. H. Freeman.

23 Described in depth in Aben and de Wit, *The Enclosed Garden*.

24 Ibid.

25 André Chevrillon, *Marrakech dans les Palmes*, 1913, p. 239. From Quentin Wilbaux and Kirk McElhearn, *Marrakesh: The Secret of Courtyard Houses*, 2000, Paris: ACR Edition.

26 Magda Sibley, in Edwards *et al.*, *Courtyard Housing*.

27 Souk – term for a commercial zone, market area.

4 Ritual and emptiness – and the rigour of developing an idea

1 François Cali, author of *L'Ordre Cistercien*, 2005, Paris: Fernand Hazan.

2 Megan Cassidy-Welch suggests that the cloister represents *earthly* paradise through the architecture (Jerusalem), and *heavenly* paradise, equated with the garden (the Garden of Eden) (in her *Monastic Spaces and their Meanings: Thirteenth-Century English Cistercian Monastries*, 2001, Turnhout, Belgium: Brepols).

3 Ibid.

4   Sylvia Landsberg talks of the importance of the greensward. Not only is it symbolic of rebirth and everlasting life, but it also has an important psychological role. She quotes Hugh of Fouilloy 'the green turf which is in the middle of the material cloister refreshes the encloistered eyes and their (the nuns') desire to study returns.' (In her *The Medieval Garden,* 1996, London: British Museum Press.)

5   Wolfgang Braunfels, *Monasteries of Western Europe: The Architecture of the Orders,* 1973, Princeton, NJ: Princeton University Press.

6   The Dominican monastery of La Tourette, at Evreux, France, was designed by Le Corbusier, 1957–60.

7   Anton Henze, *La Tourette: The Corbusier Monastery*, 1966, London: Lund Humphries.

8   Store room or cellar.

9   Le Thoronet and its sister abbeys, Sénanque and Silvacane, were constructed around the same period, and are thought to be designed by the same team of masons.

10 Haiku by Saigyo, twelfth century, in Gunter Nitschke, *Japanese Gardens,* 2007, Cologne: Taschen, p. 14.

11 François Berthier, *Reading Zen in the Rocks: The Japanese Dry Landscape Garden,* 2000, Chicago: University of Chicago Press, p. 5.

12 Ibid., p. 41.

13 Charles Moore *et al., The Poetics of Gardens,* 1993, Cambridge, MA: MIT Press.

14 Nanzen-ji originates from the thirteenth century and has undergone many changes since. It was completely rebuilt in the sixteenth century.

15 A shoji screen, often a room divider, is rice paper stretched over a timber frame, and the screen is divided into small panels.

16 Fondazione Querini Stampalia, Venice, Italy, renovated by Carlo Scarpa, 1961–63.

17 Anne-Catrin Schultz, *Carlo Scarpa Layers*, 2007, London: Edition Axel Menges.

18 Designed by Mario De Luigi.

19 Richard Murphy, *Querini Stampalia Foundation,* 1993, London: Phaidon Press.

20 Ibid.

21 Anne-Catrin Schultz, 'Carlo Scarpa: Built Memories', in Jan Birksted, ed., *Landscapes of Memory and Experience,* 2001, London: Taylor & Francis, p. 54.

22 Ibid.

5 Sensory seclusion: the affective garden, the garden room as a scene for living

1   *Groundhog Day,* dir. Harold Ramis,1993.

2   Original description by Patrick Bowe, *Gardens of Portugal*, 1989, Lisbon: Quetzal Editores, p. 71.

3   Helen Atlee, *The Gardens of Portugal*, 2008, London: Frances Lincoln.

4   Pools are more often referred to as tanks in Portugal.

5   Steven Holl *et al.*, *Questions of Perception: Phenomenology of Architecture,* 1994, Tokyo: A+U.

6   Juhani Pallasmaa, *The Eyes of the Skin: Architecture and the Senses,* 2005, London: John Wiley.

7   Ibid.

8   Georges Didi-Huberman, 'Skyspaces', in Peter Noever, ed., *James Turrell: The Other Horizon,* 1999, Vienna: MAK.

9   The Benedictine Monastery of the Holy Trinity at Las Condes, Santiago, was first designed in 1954 by Arturo Baeza, Alberto Cruz and Jose Vial, and the second design by Gabriel Guarda, Martin Correa and Patricio Gross (collaborator).

10   Piet Oudolf, Landscape Designer, and pioneer of the *new perennial* movement in planting and landscape design. John Coke, Plantsman.

11   An oast house is a traditional farm building in the south of England designed specifically for the drying of hops for the brewing process.

12   Victoria Rosner, *Modernism and the Architecture of Private Life,* 2005, New York: Columbia University Press.

13   It was a topic much discussed by the Bloomsbury Group, writers, artists and intellectuals, in the early twentieth century. Members of the group such as Vanessa Bell and Virginia Woolf both experimented through painting and literature, challenging the restrictions of their childhood. E. M. Forster's novel *Howards End* (1910) focuses around the house.

14   Jane Brown, *Sissinghurst: Portrait of a Garden,* 1994, London: Orion Publishing.

15   Ibid. This was in part born out of necessity with the small amount of habitable space available.

16   Its name and proportions derive from the interior of the vernacular Kent oast house, seen also at Bury Court.

6 Detachment: the separation of the garden from the building

1   The design of Villa Lante, started in the mid-sixteenth century, is attributed to Giacomo Barozzi da Vignola.

2   The town was reshaped in the 1560s with a new 'trident' formation of streets, reinforcing the importance and influence of the Cardinal Gambara who had chosen to create his summer residence here on the old hunting ground. The design makes a connection between City and Nature, Architecture and Landscape, and is attributed to Vignola, although it was worked on over subsequent periods, depending on the changing fortunes of the owners. See Van der Ree *et al.*, *Italian Villas and Gardens,* 1992, Munich: Prestel.

3   Parterre - literally meaning *on the ground* (French fifteenth century), a level garden, often square or rectilinear, comprising ornamental geometric patterns through the arrangement of the planting, and edged with stone, gravel or clipped hedges such as box.

4   Casino – a small summerhouse.

5   Elizabeth Barlow Rogers, *Landscape Design: A Cultural and Architectural History,* 2001, New York: Harry N. Abrams.

6   Frances Hodgson Burnett, *The Secret Garden,* 1911.

7   Jennifer Potter, *Secret Gardens,* 1998, London: Conran Octopus.

8   Mottisfont House, designed by Hampshire County Architects Department, Winchester, led by Sir Colin Stansfield-Smith.

9   The Garden of Exile and Emigration at the Jewish Museum was designed by Daniel Libeskind, 1998, opened in 2001.

10 Daniel Libeskind, 1999: http://www.helium.com/items/1343488-daniel-libeskind-jewish-museum?page=3 Accessed 29 June 2011.

11 Office architects Kersten Geers and David van Severen, Belgium.

12 Jane Smiley, *Duplicate Keys*, 1996, London: Flamingo.

13 Mary Soderstrom, *Recreating Eden: A Natural History of Botanical Gardens*, 2001, Montreal: Véhicule Press.

14 John Harvey, *Medieval Gardens,* 1990, London: B. T. Batsford.

15 The geometric patterning such as bi-symmetry and the spiral, found in the formation and development of plants.

16 John Prest, *The Garden of Eden, the Botanic Garden and the Re-creation of Paradise*, 1981, New Haven, CT: Yale University Press, p. 6.

17 Wakehurst Place in West Sussex, UK, a branch of Royal Botanic Gardens, Kew, is a plant conservation project, housing one of the largest seed banks in the world.

18 Founded by Sir Henry Danvers in 1621, who gave the university £5,000 for a physic garden 'whereby learning might be improved'. Louise Allen, Foreword, *The Family Beds*, Alison Turnbull, 2005, London: The Linnean Society.

19 Designed by Inigo Jones and executed by his master-mason Nicholas Stone in 1682.

20 Pinery – beds for growing pineapples.

21 An affectation of the French *potager,* meaning kitchen garden.

22 Such as Virgil's *Georgics* and works by Pliny the Younger.

23 Gazebo – a shelter or kiosk in a garden for sitting in.

24 Owned by English Heritage.

25 It is currently run by Garden Organic, the working name for the Henry Doubleday Research Association, a national charity for organic growing. It is being developed by a team of gardeners, and is now an exemplar for gardening techniques and production today.

Selected bibliography

Aben, Rob & Saskia de Wit (1999). *The Enclosed Garden*. Rotterdam: 010 Publishers.

Atlee, Helena (2008). *The Gardens of Portugal*. London: Frances Lincoln.

Atlee, Helena (2010). *The Gardens of Japan*. London: Frances Lincoln.

Austen, Jane (1818). *Northanger Abbey*. London: John Murray.

Barlow Rogers, Elizabeth (2001). *Landscape Design: A Cultural and Architectural History*. New York: Harry N. Abrams.

Bathrick, David, Brad Prager & Michael David Richardson (2008). *Visualizing the Holocaust: Documents, Aesthetics, Memory*. London: Camden House.

Benvolo, Leonardo (1980). *The History of the City*. London: Scolar Press.

Berthier, François (2000). *Reading Zen in the Rocks: The Japanese Dry Landscape Garden*. Chicago: University of Chicago Press.

Billington, Jill (2003). *London's Parks and Gardens*. Singapore: Tien Wah Press.

Birkstead, Jan (ed.) (2001). *Landscapes of Memory and Experience*. London: Taylor & Francis.

Bowe, Patrick (1989). *Gardens of Portugal*. Lisbon: Quetzal Editores.

Bradley-Hole, Christopher (2007). *Making the Modern Garden*. London: Mitchell Beazley.

Braunfels, Wolfgang (1973). *Monasteries of Western Europe: The Architecture of the Orders*. Princeton, NJ: Princeton University Press.

Breitschmid, Markus (2008). *The Significance of the Idea in the Architecture of Valerio Olgiati*. Zurich: Verlag Niggli AG, Sulgen.

Brown, Jane (1994). *Sissinghurst: Portrait of a Garden*. London: Orion Publishing.

Bruno, Francisco, Maria Daroca, Yllescas Ortiz & Felipe de la Fente Darder (2003). *Córdoba: An Architectural Guide*. Cordoba: Colegio Ofical de Arquitectos de Córdoba.

Caldwell, Ellen M. (1991). '*An Architecture of the Self, New Metaphors for Monastic Enclosure*'. *Essays in Medieval Studies* 8: www.illinoismedieval.org/ems/vol8/caldwell. Accessed 2 May 2011.

Cali, François (2005). *L'Ordre Cistercien*. Paris: Fernand Hazan.

Carita, Helder & Homen Cardoso (April 1991). *Portuguese Gardens*. Woodbridge, Suffolk, UK: Antique Collectors' Club.

Carroll, Maureen (2003). *Earthly Paradises*. London: British Museum Press.

Cassidy-Welch, Megan (2001). *Monastic Spaces and their Meanings: Thirteenth-Century English Cistercian Monasteries*. Turnhout, Belgium: Brepols.

Chevrillon, André (1913). *Marrakech dans les Palmes*. In Quentin Wilbaux and Kirk McElhearn, *Marrakesh: The Secret of Courtyard Houses* (2000), Paris: ACR Edition.

Clark, Emma (2004). *The Art of the Islamic Garden*. Marlborough, Wilts: Crowood Press.

Coffin, David R. (1971). *The Study and History of the Italian Garden*. Washington, DC: Dumbarton Oaks.

D'Avoine, Pierre & Clare Melhuish (2005). *Housey Housey: A Pattern Book of Ideal Homes*. London: Black Dog Press.

Didi-Hubermann, Georges (1999). 'Skyspaces' in Peter Noever (ed.) *James Turrell: The other horizon*, Vienna: MAK.

Edwards, Brian, Magda Sibley, Mohamad Hakmi & Peter Land (2005).*Courtyard Housing: Past Present and Future*. London: Taylor & Francis.

El-Shorbagy, Abdel-moniem (2010). 'Traditional Islamic-Arab House: Vocabulary and Syntax'. *International Journal of Civil and Environmental Engineering* (IJCEE-IJENS) 10(4): www.waset.org/journals/ijcee/ Retrieved 2 May 2011.

Erlande-Branenburg, Alain & Nicholas Buant (2008). *Senanque, Silvacane, Le Thoronet: Trois Soeurs Cisterciennes en Provence*. Paris: Editions Huitiemejour.

Esposito, Antonio & Giovani Leoni (2003). *Eduardo Souto De Moura*. Milan: Electa.

Esquieu, Yves (2006). *Le Thoronet, Une Abbaye Cistercienne*. Arles/Paris: Cite de L'Architecture et Patrimoine Artisteas/Actes Sud.

Fairchild Ruggles, D. (2008). *Islamic Gardens and Landscapes*. Philadelphia: University of Pennsylvania Press.

Farrar, Linda (1998). *Ancient Roman Gardens*. Stroud, Glos.: Budding Books.

Fathy, Hassan (1986). *Natural Energy and Vernacular Architecture: Principles and Examples with Reference to Hot Arid Climates*. Chicago: University of Chicago Press.

Girouard, Mark (1985). *Cities and People*. New Haven, CT: Yale University Press.

Graham, Dorothy (1938). *Chinese Gardens. Gardens of the Contemporary Scene: An Account of their Design and Symbolism*. New York: Dodd, Mead.

Gregotti, Vittorio (1979). 'Editorial', *Rassegna*, 1 Dec. 1979, 6.

Harvey, John (1990). *Medieval Gardens*. London: B. T. Batsford.

Hayakawa Masao (1973). *The Garden Art of Japan*. Chicago: Art Media Resources.

Henze, Anton (1966). *La Tourette: The Corbusier Monastery*. London: Lund Humphries.

Hobhouse, Penelope (2002). *The Story of Gardening*. London: Dorling Kindersley.

Hodgson, Frances Burnett (1911). *The Secret Garden*. London: Puffin Classics.

Holl, Steven, Juhani Pallasmaa & Alberto Pérez Gómez (1994). *Questions of Perception. Phenomenology of Architecture*. Tokyo: A+U.

Jashemski, Wilhelmina F. (1981). 'The Campanian Peristyle Garden'. In Elizabeth MacDougall & Wilhelmina F. Jashemski (eds) *Ancient Roman Gardens*. Washington, DC: Dumbarton Oaks.

Jekyll, Gertrude (1843–1932). *Wall and Water Gardens*. London: Country Life.

Jenks, Charles, & Edwin Heathcote (2010). *The Architecture of Hope. Maggie's Cancer Caring Centres*. London: Frances Lincoln.

Jennings, Anne (2004). *Medieval Gardens*. London: English Heritage.

Jones, Edward & Christopher Woodward (1983). *A Guide to the Architecture of London*. London: Weidenfeld and Nicolson.

Keswick, Maggie (1978).*The Chinese Garden*. London: Academy Editions.

Kirkwood, Niall (ed.) (2001). *Manufactured Sites: Rethinking the Post-Industrial Landscape*. London: Taylor & Francis.

Kuitert, Wybe (2002). *Themes in the History of Japanese Garden Art*. Honolulu: University of Hawaii Press.

Landsberg, Sylvia (1996).*The Medieval Garden*. London: British Museum Press.

Lehman, Jonas (1980) *Earthly Paradise Garden and Courtyard in Islam*. London: Thames and Hudson.

Leroux-Dhuys, Jean-François (1998). *Cistercian Abbeys: History and Architecture*. Cologne: Konemann.

Liedtke, Peter (2004). 'Sintering Bunker Garden'. In Peter Reed (ed.) *Groundswell: Constructing the Contemporary Landscape*. New York: The Museum of Modern Art.

Los, Sergio (1993). *Carlo Scarpa*. Cologne: Benedkt Taschen.

MacDougall, Elisabeth B. & Richard Ettinghausen (eds) (1976). *The Islamic Garden*. Washington, DC: Dumbarton Oaks.

Mann, William A. (1981). *Space and Time in Landscape Architectural History*. New York: Landscape Architecture.

Masson, Georgina (2010). *Italian Gardens*. London: Garden Art Press.

Michaels, Anne (2009). *The Winter Vault*. London: Bloomsbury.

Moore, Charles, William J. Mitchell & William Turnbull, Jr (1993). *The Poetics of Gardens*. Cambridge MA: MIT Press.

Moynihan, Elizabeth B. (1979). *Paradise as a Garden*. London: Scolar Press.

Murphy, Richard (1993). *Querini Stampalia Foundation*. London: Phaidon Press.

Nitschke, Gunter (2007). *Japanese Gardens*, Cologne: Tascher.

Pallasmaa, Juhani (2005). *The Eyes of the Skin: Architecture and the Senses*. London: John Wiley.

Perez de Arce, Rodrigo & Fernando Perez Oyarzun (2003). *Valparaiso School Open City Group*. Basel: Birkhauser Verlag.

Pfeifer Gunter & Per Brauneck (2008). *Courtyard Houses A Housing Typology*. Basel: Birkhauser.

Postiglione, Gennaro (ed.) (2008). *One Hundred Houses for One Hundred European Architects of the Twentieth Century*, Cologne: Taschen.

Potter, Jennifer (1998). *Secret Gardens*. London: Conran Octopus.

Prest, John (1981). *The Garden of Eden, the Botanic Garden and the Re-creation of Paradise*. New Haven, CT: Yale University Press

Reynolds, John S. (2002). *Courtyards: Aesthetic, Social, and Thermal Delight*. New York: John Wiley.

Rosner, Victoria (2005). *Modernism and the Architecture of Modern Life*, New York: Columbia University Press.

Scheindlin, Raymond P., tr., Masoret (1995). 5(1): 3. From Roald Hoffmann and Shira Leibowitz Schmidt, *Old Wines New Flasks: Reflections on Science and the Jewish Tradition*. New York: W. H. Freeman.

Schulz, Anne-Catrin (2007). *Carlo Scarpa Layers*, London: Edition Axel Menges.

Shepherd, John Chiene & Geoffrey Alan Jellicoe (1966). *Italian Gardens of the Renaissance*. London: Tiranti Library.

Simons, Walter (2001). *Cities of Ladies: Beguine Communities in the Medieval Low Countries, 1200–1565*, Philadelphia, PA: University of Philadelphia Press.

Soderstrom, Mary (2001). *Recreating Eden: A Natural History of Botanical Gardens*. Montreal: Véhicule Press.

Sullivan, Chip (2002). *Garden and Climate*. New York: McGraw-Hill.

Summerson, John (1969). *The Architecture of the Eighteenth Century*. London: Thames and Hudson.

Sullivan, Chip (2002). *Garden and Climate*. New York: McGraw-Hill.

Tate, Alan (2001). *Great City Parks*. London: Taylor & Francis.

Teasdale, W. (1993). 'A Glimpse of Paradise: Monastic Space and Inner Transformation'. *Parabola* 18. New York: Parabola.

Turnbull, Alison (2005). *The Family Beds*. London: The Linnean Society.

Van der Ree, Paul, Gerit Smienk & Clemens Steenbergen (1992). *Italian Villas and Gardens*. Munich: Prestel.

Wharton, Edith (1904). *Italian Villas and their Gardens*. New York: The Century Co.

Zelizer, Barbie (2000). *Visual Culture and the Holocaust*. London: Athlone Press.

Illustration credits

All illustrations not credited below are courtesy of Kate Baker.

Introduction

0.1   Persian Carpet 1670–1750
      Courtesy of the Victoria and Albert Museum, UK

1 Defining the territory: the ambiguous nature of an enclosed garden

1.1   Fisherman's allotment, Wimmenummer Duinen, Egmond aan Zee,
      North Holland
      Courtesy of Walter Herfst
1.15 The Machuca Patio, Alhambra, Granada, Spain
      Courtesy of Belinda Mitchell
1.16 Abbey Gardens, Tresco, UK
      Courtesy of Jennifer Andrews
1.18 Santi Quatro Coronatti, Rome
      Courtesy of Sam Johnston
1.19 Santi Quatro Coronatti, Rome, ground floor plan
      Drawn by Mark West/Author
1.20 Simplified plan of Santi Quatro Coronatti, Rome
      Drawn by Mark West
1.28 Amber Palace, Jaipur, India
      Courtesy of Karl Gemertsfelder

1.35 Mesquite, Court of Oranges, Cordoba
      Courtesy of Nick Timms
1.36 Rows of columns inside the Mesquite
      Courtesy of Katy Blott
1.38 Mesquite, Cordoba, ground floor plan
      Drawn by Mark West/Author
1.39 Plan of St Gall
      Based on plan reproduced in J. M. Richards, *Abbeys*, 1968,
      The Hamlyn Publishing Group.
1.41 Bird's eye view of the Generalife
      Courtesy of Moore, Mitchell and Turnbull, *The Poetics of Gardens*,
      1993, MIT Press.
1.42 Patio del Ciprés de la Sultana
      Courtesy of Belinda Mitchell
1.44 and 1.45   Duisburg-Nord Landscape Park
      Courtesy of Vinesh Pomal

2 From patio to park: the enclosed garden as a generator of architectural and landscape design

2.4 and 2.5   Lakeside Villa, plan and images
      Courtesy of Office KGDVS
2.7   Atelier Bardill
      Courtesy of Archive Olgiati
2.8   Atelier Bardill, plan
      Drawn by Mark West
2.9   Atelier Bardill
      Courtesy of Archive Olgiati
2.11 Matosinhos, plan
      Drawn by Mark West/Author
2.12 Matosinhos, courtyard housing
      Courtesy of Luís Ferreira Alves
2.14 The White House, ground floor plans
      Drawn by Mark West/Author
2.19 Ground floor plan of the Maggie's Centre, London
      Courtesy of Rogers Stirk Harbour + Partners
2.22 Ground floor plan of Clare Hall, Cambridge, UK
      Drawn by Mark West/Author
2.25 Plan of the Certosa at Pavia
      Drawn by Khalid Saleh

2.29 Aerial view of St John's College
© 2011 Google – © 2011 DigitalGlobe, GeoEye, Infoterra Ltd &
Bluesky, Getmapping plc, The Geoinformation Group, Map data
© 2011 Tele Atlas

2.32 School of Music, Polytechnic Institute, Lisbon
From archi news10 2008

2.35 Louis-Jeantet Institute, Geneva, plan
Drawn by Mark West

2.37 Louis-Jeantet Institute, Geneva
Jean-Michel Landency

2.39 and 2.40 Museum of Contemporary Art, Chiado, Lisbon
Courtesy of Miguel Seabra

2.41 Palais Royal, Paris
Google Imagery © 2011, DigitalGlobe, Aerodata International
Surveys, The Geoinformation Group, | Cnes/Spot Image, IGN –
France, Map data ©2011

2.48 and 2.49 Begijnhof, Amsterdam
Courtesy of Bryony Whitmarsh

2.50 Begijnhof, Amsterdam
Adapted from © 2011 Google – The Geoinformation Group,
GeoEye, Aerodata International Surveys, Map Data © 2011 Google

3 Taming nature – and the way to paradise

3.6 Detail of the Fra Mauro map of the world
Courtesy of mapsorama www.mapsorama.com

3.8 Roman town house, typical layout
Drawn by Mark West

3.11 Pompeii, plan of the House of Faun
Drawn by Mark West

3.12 Plan of Pompeii
Adapted from image in Linda Farrar, *Ancient Roman Gardens*,
1998, Budding Books (Sutton Publishing).

3.13 Aerial view of the town of Pavia
© 2011 Google – © 2011 DigitalGlobe, Cnes/Spot Image, GeoEye,
Map data © 2011 Tele Atlas

3.14 *The Little Garden of Paradise*. Upper Rheinish Master *c.*1410
Courtesy of Städel Museum, Frankfurt

3.15 *The Annunciation* by Domenico Veneziana (1442–48)
Courtesy of Fitzwilliam Museum, Cambridge

3.16 Lutenist and singers in garden. Illustration of the *Roman de la Rose*
Courtesy of the British Library

3.19   Prince (Babur) in a garden presented with a jungle-fowl
       Courtesy of the British Museum (BM ref AN105740001)
3.20   Plan of the basic layout of the Chahar Bagh
       Courtesy of Khalid Saleh
3.23 and 3.24   Plans of the Nazrid Palaces
       Courtesy of Khalid Saleh/Author
3.33   Aerial view of Marrakech
       Courtesy of Yann Arthus-Bertrand/CORBIS
3.34   Marrakech
       Courtesy of Nick Timms

4 Ritual and emptiness – and the rigour
   of developing an idea

4.4   St Benoit sur Loire
       Courtesy of Editions Grand Moisenay-le-Petit
4.5   Standard layout for a Cistercian monastery
       After Aubert and Dimier
4.6   Central enclosed space
       Drawn by Mark West
4.8   Le Thoronet
       © 2011 Google – Imagery ©2011 DigitalGlobe, GeoEye, Cnes/
       Spot Image, IGN – France, Map Data ©2011 Tele Atlas
4.11   Le Thoronet, general arrangement
       Drawn by Mark West
4.12   Le Thoronet, cloister
       Drawn by Mark West/Author
4.13   Diagram of Geometrics
       Drawn by Mark West
4.22   Ryoan-ji, Kyoto, Japan
       From Moore, Mitchell and Turnbull, *The Poetics of Gardens*, 1993,
       MIT Press.
4.23   Ryoan-ji, view
       Courtesy of Alan Matlock
4.24   Ryoan-ji, detail
       Courtesy of Alan Matlock
4.25   Shoden-ji
       Courtesy of Kiguma. Plate
4.26   Nanzen-ji, looking out to the Hojo Garden
       Courtesy of Alan Matlock
4.27   Nanzen-ji, detail of sliding screens
       Courtesy of John Hill

4.28 Nanzen-ji, detail of rock and raked sand
Courtesy of Alan Matlock

4.30 Querini Stampalia Foundation
Courtesy of Anna Cady

4.31 Querini Stampalia Foundation, Venice
Drawn by Mark West/Author

4.32 Querini Stampalia Foundation, approach to the garden
Courtesy of Mary Ann Steane

4.33 Querini Stampalia Foundation, looking toward the screen
Courtesy of Belinda Mitchell

4.34 Querini Stampalia Foundation, looking back to the entrance
Courtesy of Anna Cady

4.35 Querini Stampalia Foundation, the screen
Courtesy of Anna Cady

4.36 Querini Stampalia Foundation, the path is completed with stepping-stones
Courtesy of Belinda Mitchell

4.37 Querini Stampalia Foundation, detail of marble sculpture
Courtesy of Anna Cady

4.38 Querini Stampalia Foundation, water spout
Courtesy of Anna Cady

5 Sensory seclusion: the affective garden, the garden room as a scene for living

5.2 Quinta da Bacalhoa, plan of gardens
Courtesy of Gaelle Goregues

5.7 Querini Stampalia garden
Courtesy of Paul Clough

5.9 Section through Turrell's Skyspace room
From Georges Didi-Huberman, 'Skyspaces', in Peter Noever, ed., *James Turrell: The Other Horizon,* 1999, Vienna: MAK

5.14 Las Condes site layout
After Valparaiso School Open City Group

5.22 Bury Court site layout
Drawn by Mark West/Author

5.23 Bury Court schematic plan
Drawn by Mark West

5.25 Looking across one of the main flower beds
Courtesy Anna Cady

5.29 Viana Palace ground floor plan
Drawn by Mark West/Author

5.30 Simplified plan
     Drawn by Mark West
5.36 Sissinghurst site layout
     Drawn by Mark West/Author
5.37 Diagrammatic Analysis
     Drawn by Mark West
5.41 Sissinghurst. White Garden
     Courtesy of Pilager

6 Detachment: the separation of the garden from the building

6.6 Overview of the Villa Lante
    From Moore, Mitchell and Turnbull, *The Poetics of Gardens*, 1993,
    MIT Press.
6.9 Dean Garnier Garden, plan
    Drawn by Mark West/Author
6.13 Garden of Exile and Emigration, Jewish Museum, Berlin,
     aerial view
     © 2011 Google – imagery 2011 DigitalGlobe, GeoContent,
     AeroWest, GeoEye, Map data © 2011 Google, Tele Atlas
6.14 and 6.15 Garden of Exile and Emigration
     Courtesy of George Middleton-Baker
6.16 Plan for the border between Mexico and the USA
     Courtesy of Office KGDVS
6.17 Border between Mexico and the USA, image
     Courtesy of Office KGDVS
6.18, 6.19 and 6.20 Padua Botanic Garden
     Courtesy of the Botanic Garden, Padua
6.21 Oxford Botanic Garden
     Courtesy of the Science Museum
6.24 Trengwainton kitchen garden, Cornwall, UK
     Courtesy of Jennifer Andrews
6.28 Audley End, UK
     Adapted from © 2011 Google – imagery © 2011 DigitalGlobe,
     Infoterra Ltd and Bluesky, GoeEye, Getmapping plc,
     The Geoinformation Group, Map data © 2011 Tele Atlas
6.29 Audley End, kitchen garden
     Courtesy of Author (with acknowledgement to English Heritage)

Index

Note: page numbers in *italic* refer to illustrations.

Agence TER 56
Al Andalus 86
Alhambra *10*, *84*, 86, 88, 90–2; Court of the Lions 89–90, *91*; Court of the Myrtles 88–9, *90*; Machuca Patio *12*; Mexuar Patio 88, *89*; Partal Gardens 91–2, *92*, *136*; site plans *87*, *88*; tiles *140*; *see also* Generalife Gardens
ambiguity of enclosure 1, 8, 34
apartments 100–2, *102*
architecture: detail and pattern *137*, 139, *139*, *140*; in the landscape 2, 3, 8, 109–10; and qualities of space 105, 108, 109; *see also* Cistercian architecture; housing design
aspect and temperature 26, 181, *181*, 184
As-Suhaymi house, Cairo 23, *23*
Atacama Desert: quebradas 69–70, *70*, *71*, 72, *72*
Atelier Bardill, Switzerland 38, *39*, 40, *40*
Audley End, Essex 183–4, *183*, *184*, *185*
Austen, Jane: *Northanger Abbey* 180
Avignon Cathedral *19*
Avoine, Pierre d' 42
axes 164
axial 75
axis 160

Babylonians 74
Bagnaia, Italy 159, *160*
Bedford Square, London 62–3, *63*
Begijnhof, Amsterdam 64, 66–7, *66*, *67*
Berthier, François 120
Bloomsbury, London 62
border control point, USA 172–3, *173*
botanic gardens 26, 165, 173, 174–6, 186; Oxford 178–9, *178*, *179*; Padua 176–8, *176*, *177*
Braunfels, Wolfgang 108
Braz da Albuquerque 132, 134
Buddhism 18
Burnett, Frances Hodgson 165
Bury Court, Surry 144–7, *145*, *146*, *147*
bunker 32, 33, 34, *33*

Cairo: As-Suhaymi house 23, *23*
Cali, François 103
Cambridge: Clare Hall 48–50, *48*, *49*; Little St Mary's churchyard 169–70, *169*; Westcott House *16* St John's College 51–4 *52*, *53*
Carrilho da Graça, João Luís 54
Carthusian Order *51*
casa patio 99
Chahar Bagh 83–5, *86*, 92
China 18
Christian gardens 18, 79, *80*, 81; *see also* cloisters

Cistercian architecture *11*, 106–8, *108*; cloisters compared to Zen gardens 117, 123; *see also* Le Thoronet monastery

Clare Hall, Cambridge 48–50, *48*, *49*

climate control 20, 175; air movement 22–3, 26, 135; aspect and temperature 26, 181, *181*, 184; humidity 23–4, 137; sun and shade 20–2; water conservation 11, 24

cloisters 1, 15, 18; architectural function 106, *107*; aspect and temperature 26; Avignon Cathedral *19*; compared to Zen gardens 117, 123; gardens 106; Pavia, Italy 50, *50*, 51, 54; siting of wash-houses 11, *11*, 106; *see also* Las Condes Monastery, Santiago; Le Thoronet monastery

colleges 51; Clare Hall 48–50, *48*, *49*; St John's, Cambridge 51–2, *52*, *53*, 54

colonnades 15, *15*, *16*, 138; depiction of the Annunciation 79, *80*; Islamic courtyards and gardens 85, 88, 93; kitchen gardens 183; peristyle gardens 76, *76*; Villa Lante 163

connected spaces 14

containment 16–20, *16*

cooling 22–3, *22*, *136*

Cordoba 99, 100–2; Mesquite *13*, 24–5, *25*, *26*; patio gardens *9*, *22*, 99–100, *100*, *101*; *see also* Viana Palace, Cordoba

Court of Oranges 24–5

Cripps Building, Cambridge *52*, *53*

Cyrus the Great 74

Dar Bouhellal, Fez *93*

Dean Garnier Garden, Winchester 166–7, *167*, *168*

design continuity between exterior and interior 25, *25*, 35, 38

detached gardens 163–4; hidden gardens 164–7, 174; memorials and remembrance 169–72; neutralising territory 172–3; *see also* botanic gardens; kitchen gardens

Docklands 30

Domenico Veneziana *80*

Duisburg-Nord Landscape Park 32–3, *33*, *34*

Earthly Paradise 83, 86

Eden 73, *74*, 106, 175

emotions 162–3, 165, 169

environmental control *see* climate control

Erskine, Ralph 48

espaliered trees 181, *181*, 184

Exile and Emigration, Garden of, Berlin 170–2, *171*, *172*

expansion and enclosure 50–4

experiential approaches 1–2, 3; Atacama Desert 69–70; Le Thoronet monastery 103, 105; Mottisfont Abbey 5–6; Quinta da Bacalhoa 131–2; Villa Lante 159–63; *see also* sensory experience

Falchetta, Piero 73

Fez: Dar Bouhellal *93*

Flaneur 64

fountains: Alhambra 89, *90*; Clare College 49–50; Islamic design 24, 83, *85*, 93; kitchen gardens 183; Roman Gardens 77; Villa Lante 159–60, 163

Fra Mauro map of the world 73, *74*

Gabirol, Solomon ibn 86

Garden of Eden 73, *74*, 106, 175

Garden of Exile and Emigration *see* sensory experience

Generalife Gardens 27–30, *28*, *29*, *30*, 86, *87*

Geneva: Louis-Jeantet Research Institute 56–8, *56*, *57*

genius loci 27, 135

generic plan 107, 109

geometry 2, 18; Atelier Bardill 38; Islamic design 82, 83, 88, 93, *97*, 175; Lakeside Villa 36, 37; Le Thoronet 110, *111–12*; offsetting natural forms 139; Quinta da Bacalhoa 133

glasshouses 174, 181, 184, *185*

Granada *see* Alhambra

green roofs 54

hedges 12, 13

herbariums 51

Hidcote Manor 8, *8*

hidden gardens (*giardinos segretos*) 164–5, 174, 186; in towns 165–7; Villa Lante 162–3

holes in the wall 13–14; Lisbon National Museum of Contemporary Art 59, *59*

Holl, Steven 135

horizontal plane 10–11

horticulture 20; *see also* botanic gardens; kitchen gardens

hortus conclusus i, 78–82, 175

hortus delicarium 82

housing design: characteristics of rooms 9–10; conventions challenged by Sissinghurst 152; courtyard

houses *21*, 92–3, *93*, *97*, 99–102, *100*, *101*; Lakeside Villa 36–7, *36*, *37*; outdoor rooms *17*, 35; Roman 75–8, *75*, *76*, *77*; semi-detached 42–5, *43*, *44*; terraces 40–2, *41*; views 3
humidity 23–4, 137

idea of captured landscape 6, *7*, 8–9, *9*
Inns of Court, London 63–4, *64*, *65*
irrigation 24, *24*, 70, *71*
Islamic gardens 2–3, *3*, 10–11, 175; influence 81; Ménara Gardens *12*; Mesquite, Cordoba *13*; paradise gardens 18, *19*, 79, 82–5; *see also* Alhambra; Generalife Gardens; Marrakech
Islamic houses 92–3, *93*, 95, 99–100
Isle of Wight *7*

Jaipur: Amber Palace *19*
Japan: Zen temples 121; *see also* Zen gardens
Jekyll, Gertrude 9
Jencks, Charles 45, 47
Jewish Museum, Berlin 170–2, *170*, *171*, *172*

Keswick, Maggie 45
Kiosk *12*
kitchen gardens 26–7, 174, 180–6, 186
Kyoto: Nanzen-ji Temple 121–3, *122*, *123*; Ryoan-ji Temple 117, *118*, 119–20, *119*, 130; Shoden-ji Temple 120–1, *121*

Lakeside Villa, Belgium 36–7, *36*, *37*
Las Condes Monastery, Santiago 141–4, *141*, *142*, *143*, *144*
Latz, Peter 32
Le Corbusier 108
Les Alpilles, France *7*
Le Thoronet monastery 103, *104*, 105, *107*, 108–9, 113–16; compared to Fondazione Querini Stampalia 130; site and plans 109–10, *109*, *110*, *111*, *112*
Lincoln's Inn Fields 60
Lisbon: Lusiada University 15, *16*; National Museum of Contemporary Art 58–9, *58*, *59*; Polytechnic Institute School of Music 54, *55*, *56*
Little St Mary's churchyard, Cambridge 169–70, *169*
London: evolved spaces 63–4, *64*, *65*; garden squares 62–3, *63*; Phoenix garden 165, *166*; The White House 42–3, *43*, *44*, 45

Louis-Jeantet Research Institute, Geneva 56–8, *56*, *57*
Lusiada University, Lisbon 15, *16*

Maggie's Centre, Charing Cross Hospital, UK 45, *46*, 47, *47*
Maghreb 22, 93
Mappa Mundi Hereford 73
Marrakech *94*, *96*, 97, *99*, 101–2; Medersa Ben Youssef Theological College *83*; Ménara Gardens *12*; riad courtyards *11*, *21*, 93, *94*, 95, *97*, *98*; souk 93, 95, *95*
Matosinhos, Portugal 40
meadows: roof garden 54, *55*, *56*
Medersa Ben Youssef Theological College, Marrakech *83*
medieval gardens 79–82, *81*
memorials and remembrance 31, 169–72
Mesopotamia 74
metaphorical space 16, 18, 82, 102, 105; Chahar Bagh 83–5
Michaels, Anne 73
microclimate 135, 175; *see also* climate control
monasteries 105–8; Pavia, Italy 50–1, *50*, *51*, 54; St Gall, Switzerland 26, *27*; *see also* cloisters; Las Condes Monastery, Santiago; Le Thoronet monastery
mosques 82; Mesquite, Cordoba *13*, 24–5, *25*, *26*
Mottisfont
murals 78
Museum of Contemporary Art, Lisbon 58–9 *58*, *59*
music studio 38, *39*, 40, *40*

Nanzen-ji Temple, Kyoto 121–3, *122*, *123*
Nazrid Palaces *see* Alhambra
Netherlands: fisherman's allotment *7*
neutralising territory 172–3
Nicolson, Harold 152

oases 69–70, 72, 73; border control point 172–3, *173*
Office: Kersten Geers David Van Severen 36, 172
Olgiati, Valerio 38, 40
Oudolf, Piet 146, 187
outdoor rooms 8–9, 35, 187; characteristics 9–10; environment *see* climate control; horizontal plane 10–11; metaphorical space 18; relationship with people 17; Renaissance gardens 164;

Sissinghurst 152, 155; Skyspace projects 138–9; utility 20; vertical plane 12–15

Oxford Botanic Garden 178–9, *178*, *179*

Padua Botanic Garden 176–8, *176*, *177*

Pairidaeza 74, 184

Palais Royal, Paris 60–2, *61*

Pallasmaa, Juhani 136, 137

paradise 45, 73, 74, 82, 106

parterres: Padua Botanic Garden 177, *177*; Quinta da Bacalhoa 133, *134*; Villa Lante 159–60, *160*

patio 41,42, *see also* Alhambra, Generalife gardens

pattern 84, 139, *139*; Islamic 2, *3*, *10*, *19*, 25; Zen gardens 120; *see also* parterres

Pavia: Carthusian monastery 50–1, *50*, *51*, 54, 106; Roman layout *78*

pavilions 11, *11*; Generalife 28–9, *28*, *30*; Hidcote Manor *8*; Quinta da Bacalhoa 132, *133*, 134, *134*, 135; Serpentine Gallery designs 187

paving 10, *10*; Islamic design 25, 82

peristyle gardens 75–8, *75*

Persian carpets 2–3, *3*

Persian gardens 74, 180

Peter Latz and Partners 32

Phoenix garden, London 165, *166*

plants: Bury Court 146–7, *147*; and humidity 24; Las Condes Monastery 143–4; Sissinghurst 156–7, *156*; *see also* botanic gardens, kitchen gardens

Pompeii *75*, *76*, *77*

pools 23; Alhambra 88, *90*, *136*; Amber Palace, Jaipur *19*; Islamic design 2, 82, *85*; Lakeside Villa *36*, 37; Querini Stampalia Foundation 126, *127*, 128; Quinta da Bacalhoa 133, *134*–5; Roman Gardens 76–7; Villa Lante 160, 163

porous walls 15, *30*

Porro, Girolamo 177–8

Portugal: Quinta da Bacalhoa 131–5, *132*, *133*, *134*; terraced houses at Matosinhos 40; see *also* Lisbon

potagers 182–3, *182*

Powell and Moya (architects) 52

public gardens in cities 60; evolved spaces 63–4, *65*; garden squares 62–3, *63*; Palais Royal, Paris 60–2, *61*; sanctuaries 64, 66–7, *66*, *67*

quebradas 69–70, *71*, 72, *72*

Querini Stampalia Foundation, Venice 123–4, *124*–*5*, 126, *126*–*7*, 128, *128*, 129; compared to Ryoan-ji and Le Thoronet 130; use of water 126, *127*, 128, *129*, *136*

Quinta da Bacalhoa, Portugal 131–5, *132*, *133*, *134*

Qur'an 82, 84, 90

reclaimed sites 30–3

refuges 45

reja 100, 101

religion and gardens 18, 79, 81, 117

Renaissance gardens 164; *see also* Villa Lante

response to site 27; Atelier Bardill 38; Generalife Gardens 27–30, *28*, *29*, *30*; Lakeside Villa 37; Las Condes Monastery 141, *142*; Matosinhos 40–1, 42; reclaimed sites 30–3

retaining wall 28, 142–3

riad courtyards *11*, *21*, 93, *94*, 95, *97*, *98*

rills 144

ritual 103, 106, 108, 144

Rogers Stirk Harbour and Partners 45

Le Roman de la Rose 81–2, *81*

Roman houses and gardens 75–8, *75*, *76*, *77*; Cordoba 99, 100

Rome: Santi Quatro Coronatti 14, *14*

roof gardens 54, *55*, *56*

ruins: industrial 32–3, *33*

rus in urbe 78

Ryoan-ji Temple, Kyoto 117, *118*, 119–20, *119*, 130

Sackville-West, Vita 152

St Benoit sur Loire *107*

St Gall, Switzerland 26, *27*

St John's College, Cambridge 51–2, *52*, *53*, 54

sanctuary 64

Santiago, Chile: Catholic University *15*; Las Condes Monastery 141–4, *141*, *142*, *143*, *144*

Santi Quatro Coronatti, Rome 14, *14*

Scarpa, Carlo 123–4, 128–9, 130

School of Music, Lisbon 54, 55, *55*, *56*

Schultz, Anne-Catrin 128–9

science 175–6

sensory experience 135–9, 152, 157; Garden of Exile and Emigration 170–1

Serpentine Gallery, London 187

shade 20, 21–2, 24, *76*, 137; Islamic houses 93; Las Condes Monastery 142, *143*, 144

Shoden-ji Temple, Kyoto 120–1, *121*

Sissinghurst Castle 152–3, *153*, 155–7, *155*, *156*; site plan *154*

Skyspace projects (Turrell) 138–9, *138*

smells 137–8
Smiley, Jane: *Duplicate Keys* 174
Song of Solomon 79
sounds 95, 135
Souto de Moura, Eduardo 40
stone: qualities of 103, 105, 108, 113, 114–15, *114*
Sung Dynasty: landscape drawings 121
sunken gardens: Louis-Jeantet Research Institute 56–8, *56*, *57*
sun and shade 20–2, *104*; Atelier Bardill 38, *40*; Le Thoronet 114, 116, *116*
Switzerland: Atelier Bardill 38, *39*, 40, *40*; St Gall monastery 26, *27*
symbolism 18, 172; plants 79, 82, 106; Zen gardens 117

takhtabush 23, *23*
temperature *136*, 137; and aspect 26, 181, *181*, 184
template, garden as earthly paradise 83
texture 135–7, *137*
Thames Barrier Park 30–2, *31*
Theatre 75
threshold gardens 56–9
tiles *84*, 95, 134, 139, *139*, *140*; for colour 82, *83*, 126
Toconao 69, *70*
Trengwainton, Cornwall: kitchen garden *181*
Tresco Abbey Gardens *13*
Turrell, James 138–9
Typology i
type 34

University of Lusiada, Lisbon 15, *16*
urban gardens *see* public gardens in cities
Utility 20

Val Joanis potager, France *182*
Venice *see* Querini Stampalia Foundation, Venice
vertical plane 12–15
vertical planning 54

Viana Palace, Cordoba 148–50, *148*, *149*, *151*, 152; ground floor plan *150*; use of tiles *138*
Victoria Embankment Gardens, London *18*
views: beyond Zen gardens *118*, 120, 121, 122; housing design 3; upwards *93*, 124, 138–9
Villa Farnese 164
Villa Lante 159–63, *160*, *161*, *162*, *163*
Virgin Mary 79, *80*
Vitruvius 76

Wakehurst Place 175–6
wall, role of the *137*, 138, 174; in kitchen gardens 180, 181
wash-house 11, *11*
water 10; and humidity 23–4; Islamic design 2, 82, 83, *85*, 88, 90, *90*; Japanese gardens 18, 117; Lakeside Villa 36–7; Las Condes Monastery 142, 144; Lisbon National Museum of Contemporary Art *58*, 59; and planting 11, 24, *24*; Querini Stampalia Foundation, Venice 126, *127*, 128, *129*, *136*; Roman gardens 76–7; Villa Lante, Italy 160–1, *161*, 163
Westcott House, Cambridge, *16*
The White House, London 42–3, *43*, *44*, 45
Wilmotte, Jean Michel 58
Winchester: Dean Garnier garden 166–7, *167*, *168*
wind protection 22, 26, 135

Xenophon 74

Zen gardens 18, 117; compared with Cistercian cloisters 117, 123; Nanzen-ji Temple 121–3, *122*, *123*; Ryoan-ji Temple 117, *118*, 119–20, *119*, 130; Shoden-ji Temple 120–1, *121*

Zumthor, Peter 187